1980

 *The Springer Series on Death and Suicide*

*ROBERT KASTENBAUM, Ph.D., Series Editor*

VOLUME ONE
## BETWEEN LIFE AND DEATH
*Robert Kastenbaum, Ph.D., Editor*

VOLUME TWO
## SUICIDE AFTER SIXTY
The Final Alternative
*Marv Miller, Ph.D.*

VOLUME THREE
## CHILDREN'S CONCEPTIONS OF DEATH
*Richard Lonetto, Ph.D.*

# Contributors

SANDRA L. BERTMAN
University of Massachusetts
Medical Center
Worcester, Massachusetts

SANDOR B. BRENT
Wayne State University
Department of Psychology
Detroit, Michigan

CHARLES A. GARFIELD
University of California
San Francisco
Cancer Research Institute
San Francisco, California

RICHARD A. KALISH
California School of
Professional Psychology
Berkeley, California

ROBERT KASTENBAUM
Cushing Hospital
Framingham, Massachusetts

RUSSELL NOYES, JR.
University of Iowa
Department of Psychiatry
Iowa City, Iowa

BARBARA ROSS
University of Massachusetts
Psychology Department
Boston, Massachusetts

SHELDON RUDERMAN
Gladman Psychosomatic
Medicine Center
Berkeley, California

# BETWEEN
# LIFE AND DEATH

Robert Kastenbaum, *Ph.D.*
*Editor*

SPRINGER PUBLISHING COMPANY
New York

Copyright © 1979 by Springer Publishing Company, Inc.

Springer Publishing Company, Inc.
200 Park Avenue South
New York, N.Y. 10003

79 80 81 82 83 / 10 9 8 7 6 5 4 3 2 1

**Library of Congress Cataloging in Publication Data**

Main entry under title:

Between life and death.

    (The Springer series on death and suicide; v. 1)
    Includes bibliographical references and index.
    1.  Death—Psychological aspects.  2.  Future life.
I.  Kastenbaum, Robert.  II.  Series: Springer series on
death and suicide; v. 1.
BF789.D4B48      155.9'37      79-17760
ISBN 0-8261-2540-9
ISBN 0-8261-2541-7 pbk.

Printed in the United States of America

# Contents

Introduction    vii

## 1
A Personal Encounter with Death
and Some Consequences
SHELDON RUDERMAN    1

## 2
Happily Ever After
ROBERT KASTENBAUM    15

## 3
The Same Old Story? A Historical Perspective
BARBARA ROSS    29

## 4
The Dying Patient's Concern with "Life After Death"
CHARLES A. GARFIELD    45

## 5
Contacting the Dead: Does Group Identification Matter?
RICHARD A. KALISH    61

## 6
Near-Death Experiences: Their Interpretation
and Significance
RUSSELL NOYES, JR.    73

### 7

Deliberately Induced, Premortem Out-of-Body Experiences:
An Experimental and Theoretical Approach
SANDOR B. BRENT                                              89

### 8

Communicating with the Dead: An Ongoing Experience
as Expressed in Art, Literature, and Song
SANDRA L. BERTMAN                                            124

### 9

Death through the Retroscopic Lens
ROBERT KASTENBAUM                                            156

# Introduction

Here they come again, those tales of commerce with the dead, those reports of strange happenings in the borderlands between the living and the who-knows-what.

But didn't science slam the door resoundingly shut a long time ago? Did somebody leave the keyhole unplugged? Those who are skeptics through and through now have new occasion to mutter about the indomitable nature of human folly and naïveté. Hmmmph! What some people will believe!

Those who are innocent of historical knowledge, however, already have concluded that the secrets of life and death have been newly revealed in this morning's headline or this afternoon's television talk show. Scientists now know what death is, you see, and the dead themselves keep coming back to tell us all about it.

People who are secure in their conclusions (fixed in either the yea or nay position) can snap this book closed immediately and spare themselves the information, observations, and, above all, the questions that follow, chapter after chapter. But others may welcome the opportunity to examine the current revival of interest in communication between living and dead through several rather perceptive sets of eyes. Several of the contributors participated in the 1977 symposium of the American Psychological Association. "Communication with the Dead: New Data or Same Old Story?" aroused such interest that we determined to make a revised version available in printed form. This has also provided the opportunity to invite several others with illuminating angles of vision to add their observations as well. Contributors to book and symposium were not selected on the basis of their belief or disbelief in particular phenomena. Emphasis instead was on their experience, scientific or clinical credentials, personal integrity, and ability to either add new information or enrich and reflect on existing information.

Many books have been published in the past few years in the general area of dying, death, and bereavement (including contributions by several of the present authors). One now has a reasonable choice of perspectives in learning about care of the terminally ill person, the prevention of suicide, the response to bereavement, and related topics. There is little up-to-date literature available, however, to provide perspective on some of the most fascinating and elusive phenomena. Raymond Moody's *Life After Life* opened the gates to an outpouring of reports that some prefer to call near-death encounters while others take them as actual returns from death. We believe these experiences, by whatever name, deserve to be taken seriously. The experiences are significant in themselves to the person who has them and to many who hear about them. They may also be significant in their impact on attitudes and behaviors well beyond the crisis-of-death situation itself. Furthermore, method and knowledge in science in general may be challenged.

This book adds specific observations to those already recorded. But it also attempts to explore links between life-death borderline phenomena and other topics, bringing the exotic and the everyday spheres of experience a little closer together. In its effort to provide information, responsible criticism, and sociohistorical context this book may be unique. You will find that it is not written in a spirit of either relentless "debunking" or pipeline-to-the-divine. We simply have some thoughts on one of humankind's most ancient concerns and would like to share them with you.

# 1

# A Personal Encounter with Death and Some Consequences

*Sheldon Ruderman*

*What is it like to be dead? Or "maybe dead"? A logical positivist might tell us that these are not proper questions. There are hidden flaws in our assumptions and use of language—we really shouldn't be asking such questions at all. But, of course, we do. Why should somebody's definition of language and logic deter us from following our curiosity, especially when it undertakes such an adventuresome journey?*

*For Sheldon Ruderman, however, it was not a matter of either idle or active curiosity. He was a man fighting for his life. Ruderman had to contend not only with the illness itself but with the (mis)treatment and the complexities of his own emotional response. In the midst of one situation he found himself in another. At the time it happened to him, the near-death experience and the out-of-body experience (OBE) that accompanied it were not generally known to the professional and lay public, and certainly not to him.*

*Ruderman's factual account of his experiences and his reflections on the impact they made on his life are a valuable human document and show us what we can still add to our understanding.*

My encounter with an advanced cancer many years ago has been a major influence in reshaping my attitude toward life. Coming through that episode, with its threat of death, has made me feel that

Adapted from a paper presented to the 85th Annual Convention of the American Psychological Association, San Francisco, 1977.

I was reborn. Why my life was spared is a question that has bothered me since.

## The Experience Begins

Early in 1959 a large chest tumor was discovered to have spread through the region of my right lung and mediastinum. Surgery revealed it to be too extensive to be operable. In response to my prodding, my surgeon reluctantly let me know that I could expect no more than two years of life. I was given an exceedingly heavy dose of radiation, which did considerably shrink the tumor. Many years later another doctor remarked that it took one miracle to survive the cancer and another to survive the radiation. That dosage subsequently proved lethal to many cancer patients. Today lung cancer patients routinely receive less than half the dosage given to me.

At the time all these medical goings on seemed unreal to me, a common emotional reaction of cancer patients given messages of doom. Nonetheless, when my new wife told me she was pregnant, I reacted strongly: She could not go through with the pregnancy. It was unfair, in my eyes, to bring a child into the world with his father so likely to leave him so soon. Inwardly, this stance upset me. I had always wanted to become a father, a state that was now seemingly within reach. My wife considered me terminally ill but she finally rejected an abortion date and went ahead with the pregnancy. This decision was to eventually save my life.

A consultation with a prominent New York specialist, one of a number of experts I had now visited, brought home the message that I was beyond medical help. Upset by his words, I walked down Park Avenue, and suddenly blood spurted out of me in all directions. I was rushed to a large medical research center. *If you can't be cured, you can at least be studied.* I was ignorant of this medical maxim until an army of white-coated young trainees kept asking me the same standardized questions daily. I began to get mad.

One day an older man without white coat and without clipboard walked in. Since he was "out of uniform," I nearly didn't recognize that he was a doctor. He asked what my life meant to me. When I shrugged off the question, he asked it twice more. I told him that I had now a specific goal, to stay alive to raise my newborn son, both for his good and for my enjoyment. I now knew that I had to live, and that this man's job was to help me.

He immediately walked out and held the first of several conversations with a surgeon who had already rejected me as a surgical possibility. Finally, the surgeon relented. Daily a profusion of orderlies, technicians, janitors, and other "small fry" trooped in to tell me that they were pulling for me. Although I was cynical about the value of good wishes, this concentrated dose of human warmth seemed to penetrate my pores. Nevertheless, medical opinion was almost unanimous that I would not survive the surgery.

The eight-hour surgery, by all accounts, was a technical marvel. The surgeon later wrote that it was the most difficult surgery of his career. Over a thousand pieces of me were extracted, including my right lung, now reduced to near charcoal by the radiation. When I came to, however, I was in another world.

Up to this time, everything that had happened fit within a conventional belief system. Now, suddenly, I felt physically battered beyond my imagination. I also felt emotionally light years away from anyone. Every question or remark I heard seemed totally irrelevant. I was very frightened and felt very, very alone. Eventually, my wife began to shorten the emotional distance between us; I don't know if I could have survived without her understanding. As my new emotional state began to be more familiar, I became aware that my mind was functioning very lucidly. I felt frightened and strange, but with a capacity to focus that I had never experienced before.

My surgeon decided I needed complete quiescence, so he ordered powerful demerol shots given approximately every three hours. I would lose consciousness almost as soon as the needle was withdrawn. This regimen was adhered to regularly for more than a week until I protested during the fifteen to twenty minutes of waking time I had between shots. It felt like annihilation. Pain, anxiety, fear—anything was better than annihilation. I implored my surgeon to stop. He promised he would do so after one or two more shots, so I ceased protesting.

When one receives a regular injection of this kind, a new biological rhythm is temporarily induced. That is, after a regular interval, a dim awareness begins to creep over you, you gradually begin to slide back toward a more conscious state, and the process becomes increasingly familiar.

Three hours after my next shot, I began to feel the familiar initial signal that the return process was about to begin. But soon it became apparent that something was wrong. I could not see. It was as if someone had enveloped me with a stack of fine meshed screens, so that just the faintest hint of light struggled through, but there were no contours of anything visible. It was almost completely dark.

It also seemed that there was a pressure on my chest. It was not unbearable, but heavy. The most striking characteristic, however, was that I had absolutely no sense of motion of my chest. I had been aware earlier that my new one-lunged breathing was quite shallow. The state I was now experiencing, however, was much more extreme. There seemed to be no breathing at all. Uncomprehending, I tried to detect any sign of motion of my chest, but it seemed totally at rest. Yet I did not experience any shortness of breath or suffocation. The urging of the biological rhythm seemed unmistakable: This was supposed to be wake-up time.

## "Maybe I Was Dead"

My mind quickly raced through a repertoire of possible explanations for this state, but every explanation had some obvious shortcoming. Something very strange was going on. I was afraid and fascinated simultaneously. Finally, a new idea occurred to me: *Maybe I was dead.* After all, I did not know what being dead was like, and maybe this was it. Certainly it would account for the nonmovement of my chest. Maybe the fight, the ordeal, was over. The end of the game.

Immediately, a powerful feeling of exhilaration swept through me. I felt free. Excitingly free. I was no longer trapped. No more fear, pain, uncertainty, whatever. Just free.

I became aware that "I" was no longer in my body. This was a little stranger than I was ready for, so I deliberately did not "look back." The fundamental rules of being now seemed up for grabs.

An old image entered by mind, that of an anthropologist, an eth-nographer, beginning to explore a new culture. At times of high anxiety, such as when I took my marital vows, I had invoked this image to allow myself the emotional security of being an observer, not the central actor, in a potentially anxiety-laden scene. So now I would chart the land of the dead.

I moved slowly around the room, speeded up, and slowed down again, experimenting with changing rates of motion very quickly. This was really fun. It seemed as if all I had to do was to think "go faster" and I was already going faster. "Reverse" was just as easy.

Then, more carefully, I moved nearer the walls and skimmed alongside. Finally, I worked up the courage to "put my hand" on the wall and push gently. My hand seemed to enter the wall. I did it again and felt myself penetrating deeper into the wall. This was a little frightening. The absence of familiar restraints can be unset-tling. I moved away from the wall again and went back to the game of speed control, which was much more fun.

A new thought was now growing in me. This free state was so much fun that there must be something wrong with it. Pleasure had always been associated with some kind of prohibition. Perhaps it seemed that anything I really enjoyed was bad for me, not allowed, a sin. This idea was now manifesting itself in my uneasiness over this strange new state of freedom.

It occurred to me, therefore, that maybe I was not dead. After all, being dead could not really be expected to be this much fun! Every-one "knew" that death was bad for you, so what I was doing now or being or whatever was in some way wrong. At no time during this state had any of my attachments to life ever occurred to me.

How to resolve the question? Well, in my belief system, dead people did not interact with live ones. If I could interact with a live person, it would mean that I was not really dead. Somehow I got back into my body. Very strenuously, I tried to get my chest to move. I tried very hard to breathe and expand my chest. If I could make someone notice, then I'd know I was not dead.

I kept working on it for some time. I was aware that some figures had looked into the room at one point and decided I was "still out," that is to say, unconscious. Finally, I heard something like "I think he's coming to." A terrific feeling of relief engulfed me. I was still alive. When I was "dead," I was exhilarated to be dead. When I was "alive," I was relieved I was alive. It was like Einsteinian relativity—I simply carried my frame of reference around with me.

I later learned that my surgeon had tired of arguing with me and decided to give me another shot while I was already out. He hadn't ever done this before, and it had never occurred to me when I was trying to understand why I couldn't regain consciousness as usual. I will return to this point later.

## A "Minor Procedure"—and Another Out-of-the-Body Experience

A few days later something apparently went wrong with the drainage in my chest. My surgeon reassured me that the "procedure" would be so minor that an injection would not be necessary. Since this was a teaching hospital, the event would be attended by about twenty-five trainees who would stand around the table. For teaching purposes the surgeon would explain each move before he made it. What he was explaining, given my limited understanding of technical jargon, sounded very much like chest surgery to me. That was obviously impossible; chest surgery requires the patient to be unconscious.

I was given a shot of novocaine or some such light painkiller. Then I felt myself being cut open along my right side. I was stunned and very confused. No one was protesting; everyone just stood around watching. The only exception was a very young girl stationed at the head of the table who was supposed to count something. Her eyes were terrified, and since her face was no more than about two feet from mine, I was very conscious of her terror. So when my surgeon asked me how I was doing, I looked at her and murmured "all right." I could not let myself contribute to that girl's terror. The torture continued.

From seemingly another part of my mind, I became aware of another characteristic of the scene. Almost none of the trainees surrounding me could actually see the mechanics of the surgery. The only possible angle for vision was from the right side of the table, but the surgeon and his assistant were there, blocking the view from the trainees on that side. Everyone else was on the wrong side of the table.

The incongruity of having assembled all these students to witness something they couldn't actually see struck me as crazy. I was unaware it was functioning to draw my attention away from the cutting of my body. It was not too hard to identify with the beings surrounding the table rather than the one on it because I had been a graduate student when my tumor was discovered. How would I see the scene if I were one of them? The only unobstructed view would have to be from above. In my mind I imagined a board, similar to a diving board, extending out from the wall in back of me. It would project over the table, and I imagined I would lie on it, belly down. In that way my line of sight would be clear.

No sooner had I imagined this scene than I found myself watching from that very point in the room, somewhere near the top. It felt perfectly normal. There was no surprise about it, no feeling of "what am I doing here?" Yet all of me was not there, since I could still feel cutting and pounding in my body. It was as if I was only half out of my body. I still experienced pain but it seemed muffled. It was as if someone had wrapped a hammer in some padding and hit me with it. That feels differently than being hit with a bare hammer. The image is not accidental: my ribs were being broken.

The surgery continued for three hours. About every twenty minutes my surgeon asked how I was doing. I had to be sufficiently in my body to answer him. I could see all the people in the room clearly. The outline of the table was less clear. The outline of my body was fuzzier still. The wound itself was a total blank. It was as if I knew I was not brave enough to look into my own body, especially as it was being cut up, because I might "faint." So I repressed seeing that part of the scene.

## Whose Definition of Reality?

At the end of the surgery, I was brought back to my bed and dumped on it like a sack of potatoes. I heard my surgeon instruct the nursing staff not to move me until I moved myself. I lay in the same position for what seemed like days. It felt as though no life was left in that body after all the trauma it had endured. My mind still functioned very clearly, but I was entirely alone in whatever mind-space I occupied. I still tried to respond to conventional communications sent my way because I was frightened of any more "life-saving" measures.

Among the characteristics of this alien mind-space was a profusion of images. Grotesque forms paraded before my eyes. Undefined, unfamiliar, nightmarish horrors. They seemed to be all over the room.

Interspersed among these grotesque images were others that were more like dreams, scenes that were just there, neither good nor bad. By now it had become obvious to me that the doctors had done all they could, but that they simply did not know enough to save my life. I was more and more sure that the question of my survival would have to be decided in some other arena, and that it had something to do with my understanding of this mind-space.

I had become aware also of a terrific pressure to define my situation coming from everyone who saw me. Did I still have a chance to live? What was the meaning of this symptom? What did this reaction mean? What other treatment was indicated? Again and again I felt the pressures of humans coping with uncertainty—and from my viewpoint losing. They constantly succumbed to the need to *feel* they understood when they clearly did not. I did not understand, either, but I knew I didn't.

It seemed to me that if I accepted any of their definitions of reality to quell my own uncertainty, many more doors would slam shut. Possibilities would be closed off, avenues that might be critical for my survival, if I could ever figure out what was happening. So I didn't protest, didn't react, didn't talk. My family was apprehensive about my withdrawn state, but I simply had to focus my complete mind to possibly understand what was happening to me. I was looking for a miracle.

Somewhere it occurred to me to face the images more squarely. They were frightening, all right, but somehow it seemed as if they might contain information. Most of the images that passed before me have long since receded from memory, but three pictures stand out to this present day.

The first occurred three times, I believe. It was a scene of a sailor being buried at sea. As I have viewed this scene in movies, the body is put on a board, a flag is draped over it, the board is tilted, and the body slides into the sea. Each time I saw the scene, the board was already tilted, the body sliding toward oblivion. It seemed clear the body was me. If nothing intervened I would be dead in less than twenty-four hours.

Each time this picture occurred, I held a conference with myself. I debated whether it was worth continuing the fight or whether I should just close my eyes and drift off to a long, long rest, out of this maelstrom. Just how much was I willing to endure to retain this tortured state of life?

Each time the question seemed to answer itself. I got an image of being in a room, backing up toward a door behind me. If I kept going, I would go through the door and be out of life. Standing in front of the door, however, was my small son, Jason. To back out the door, I would have to step on him or push him out of the way. I could not do that. So I was not free to back out the door. I had to stay and continue to fight. I resolved, therefore, that I would not close my eyes unless I promised myself to open them again. I was programming myself to stay alive.

## Santa's Image: A Surprising Key to Survival

The third image was the key to my survival. My body felt absolutely lifeless, no matter what the condition of my mind. There was no energy to move or even to talk. At this time an image of a Santa Claus bag over my right shoulder appeared. Christmas has never been a good time of year for me, so there seems to be some hidden meaning to this scene. There were no toys in the bag; instead, there were energy packets. Since I was so bereft of energy, and since this is what the bag contained, the obvious inference was to transfer some energy from the bag to me.

A nurse would come by and ask me to turn over. I neither had the energy to turn nor the energy to tell her so. At the same time I was terrified of being physically handled. In some way I felt that, given my inability to resist if I was moved in the wrong way, I would be killed by some well-meaning nurse. So "in my mind" I reached across my right shoulder with my left arm, got an energy packet, gave myself a "transfusion," and felt enough energy to turn over. After turning I was aware I was back to zero energy again. The transfusion had just covered the task, with no surplus left over. When I was asked to turn back, I repeated the whole maneuver.

After about three days I stopped trying to understand this energy source. I knew it would be there whether I understood it or not. I lived that way for approximately five weeks, drawing on an energy source outside my body. Then I began to feel my own tissue energy beginning to return. It is impossible for me to explain the difference between these subjective phenomena to anyone that has never lost this background energy in his body. The energy I experienced was coming from in back of my right shoulder; of that I am sure. Somewhere in the Castaneda-Don Juan series, Don Juan remarks that death is over the left shoulder. For whatever it is worth, I was turning over my right shoulder, and each time I received life energy.

## Some Consequences of the Experience

Other phases of this episode were also strange, but enough has been related to give the reader some flavor of it. I have been asked many times just how all this has affected my views of life, and I would like to address that question now.

I am now working as a professional counselor to clientele made up largely of cancer patients and their families. I know that confronting threats to one's life is largely a subjective matter. As a terminal patient in the eyes of a number of specialists, I should have died. There would have been no conceptual difficulty. That's what terminal patients do, don't they? It would never have been possible for anyone to see that my subjective state was really a critical variable. As it is, one doctor explains my survival by saying that I was a statistical freak, as if that really explained anything. Another, voicing a common view, neatly concludes that if I survived, I could not possibly have been a terminal patient. Therefore, the diagnosis was wrong, even if several specialists made it. Of course, my subjective awareness of the closeness of my death is completely irrelevant from this point of view. Unfortunately, terminal diagnoses of patients exist before they die, and they affect the behavior of all concerned, including the patient. A definition is not only a report of a state of existence; it is also an action that helps to shape existence. My own surgeon would never have made his contribution except for the intervention of the internist who asked me what my life meant to me.

## On a More Personal Level

The consciousness of the person who began the experience described here was very different than that of the writer of these lines, although both beings used the same name and the second continues to confront elements of the first within him. The first person was a relatively hard-line, scientific type, who related to the world analytically. If something was apparently not amenable to explanation, he tended to deny it existed: Science would eventually answer all the real or worthwhile questions of existence. He was scornful of intuitive or psychic knowledge, atheistic, and contemptuous toward any kind of mysticism, certainly toward the idea of life after death. To believe in life after death was obviously to be soft minded, a classification that, even to this day, his ego does not feel comfortable with. He was also insecure, very controlled, and used a great deal of energy to conceal a basic dislike of himself. The last trait was hidden by an exterior of education and scholarship.

The person who was reborn in the crucible of the experience, and who has been slowly emerging since, is, in a way, the very kind of person the first one always ridiculed. "I have discovered the enemy, and he is me." The altered state of consciousness that prevailed during most of my hospital stay allowed me to become aware of a kind of wider consciousness permeating the universe I am aware of. To me that consciousness is associated with a Creator who is probably neither omniscient nor omnipotent, because it is part of a wider field of consciousness, an analogue to our own existence on another scale. The problems humans have in understanding God may be partly caused by the fact that we are part of multiple consciousnesses whose purposes are not always aligned.

What is obvious to me is that I personally feel compelled to try to understand the "rules of the game."

I once would never have taken seriously the notion that "mind" meant anything more than "brain." As a result of paying closer attention to my own consciousness, it now seems to me that my brain functions more as a valve that regulates the intake of a wider consciousness. Ideas "enter" my consciousness, and I seem to have some control over the rate of their intake and to some degree over their nature. For me to begin to truly understand this multiple texture of existence often seems so "mind-blowing" that I find myself limiting the input. Altered states of consciousness continually press to break through. My internalized societally defined reaction to them pressures me to define them as normal, psychic, psychotic, creative, mystical, and so forth. But as I did in the hospital, I try to resist premature definitions of what I know I do not know.

A universe in which one becomes aware of consciousness after death has a far greater intuitive feeling of rightness to it than the more analytical egocentric belief that this life is "where it's at." Another Copernican revolution, leading to a further decentering of human beings' place in the scheme of things, seems to be in the making.

I have now experienced my own near death and have experienced others who either died or came close. It now seems to me that the dying process is analogous in some ways to the birth process. Pregnancy is a familiar concept, a "zone" between "nothing" and full-fledged birth. Spontaneously or medically, this developmental process can be aborted. We are all familiar with the swirling controversy surrounding the issue of when exactly there is a life that can be aborted.

It now seems to me that many people go through a zone of dying. The idea of a zone of being born or dying is an oversimplified way of describing a multilayered texture of consciousness states, but its simplicity makes it useful. Just as in birth, to start down that tunnel is usually to complete it, or so it appears. Sometimes, however, a person's death is "aborted" and he does not complete the journey. The people who have been interviewed by Raymond Moody and Elisabeth Kübler-Ross may be those who went a good way into that zone before returning. In my own case, when I thought I was dead, I may have been not that far down the path. The fact that I found out later a shot had been administered does not explain my mind state. I may or may not have been over-dosed. In any case, whatever it is that happened, it provided a stimulus for me to cope with this question.

I have become much more aware of the role of imagery in mental life since my experience of it in the hospital. Scientific research into the left-brain–right-brain dichotomy is beginning to tap a potential gold mine of data on cognitive processes. The visualization pro-gram pioneered by the Simontons* in Texas with cancer patients is a start on what will eventually be a major avenue of approaching the understanding of health and disease.

The ability to become more conscious of one's imaging processes is exemplified in self-hypnosis, biofeedback, dream interpretation, and meditation. Implied here is a reinterpretation of the control of or deviation from optimum health. Since my hospital experience I have come to believe that each person is the potential ultimate authority on his own being, if he so desires to be. Through an imaging, "going-inward" focus of attention, we have an early warning system of when we are heading "off the track." Instead of waiting to learn from a medical authority that one has developed a serious medical condition, it becomes possible to periodically monitor one's inner states to see if something is wrong. I am now aware of simply too many cases where a doctor has assured a pa-tient that his fears were groundless—that it was "all in his head"—and the patient was later discovered to have a large tumor.

One other personality change I wish to comment on is in the quality of interaction I now experience with other people. The pre-cancer individual using my name had a difficult time relating to people because a substantial amount of energy had to be devoted to self-protection. Of course, this is still true to an uncomfortable ex-tent. Now, however, "unreal" or superficial parrying with people hurts more inside. Although it is still a considerable problem, I am more ready to reveal vulnerability, with the implicit hope that the other will also do so, making the whole exchange take place on

---

*Carl and Stephanie Simonton are radiologists in Fort Worth, Texas, who have pio-neered an integrated program of psychotherapy and medical care for cancer patients. "Physiological self-regulation" is one of the keys to their approach.

what feels like a deeper emotional plane. When I am confronted with behavior that seems arrogant, egotistic, stingy, manipulative, and so forth, I am more aware of the corresponding characteristics in myself. It is less easy to condemn others for very long when one has an acute consciousness of participating in the same patterns. To that extent I believe I have become somewhat less moralistic and more accepting toward the range of human behavior I encounter.

Increasing openness to others leads to an intensification of experience. If a life could be measured in "units of experience," I am sure that the number of units has increased significantly since my encounter with cancer. My confrontation with death will stretch out the total experience in each calendar year of the rest of my life, however long that is going to be, after which I trust that I will be more ready to participate in a different phase of existence.

# 2

# Happily Ever After

## Robert Kastenbaum

*A century ago scientists and specialized "psychic investigators" were examining the claims of "mediums" who claimed to be receiving communications from the spirits of the deceased. This was the relatively new and controversial phenomenon of its time. Today we have our own new and controversial phenomenon: Reports that come firsthand from people who have returned to us from the threshold of death if not from death itself.*

*The following chapter (the only contribution that was not prepared expressly for this book) was written before the symposium on which this book is based and was published originally in* Human Behavior. *It represents the first attempt to place the current wave of "life-after-life" phenomena into clinical perspective. The writer was motivated by his concern that uncritical popular (and, to some extent, professional) acceptance of the reported phenomena could have unfortunate consequences for people in life-threatening circumstances. The reports play all too easily into existing patterns of wishfulfillment and media exploitation in our society. This does not mean the phenomena should be ignored, but that higher standards of critical scrutiny should be employed, not only of the data themselves but of the use we make of them.*

Haven't we all heard this story before? A man is walking briskly toward his car after attending a sporting event. Suddenly he is convulsed with pain. It is a struggle to draw breath. A moment of panic. "My God, I'm having a heart attack!"

This chapter was originally published under the title "Temptations from the Ever After" in *Human Behavior,* September, 1977, and is reprinted with permission.

Back in control. Look around. No help immediately available. Get into the car and drive to the nearest hospital myself. Will make it somehow. Keep self together despite the suffering and alarm. Pull up in front of a hospital. Up the steps and through the door with a last reserve of energy.

A nurse leaving for the day takes one look at him, and in her own alarm, says, "Mister, you ought to be in a hospital!" Smile, reply, "Now, why didn't I think of that!" Fadeout.

The actual sequence of events now involves a quick admission to the intensive care unit where the emergency team promptly assembles. His condition is precarious. The feared event occurs: The victim's heart gives out. But cardiac arrest is a challenge the team is prepared to cope with. Although in some times and places this man would now be considered dead, trained hands seek to maintain (or is it to restore?) life.

Fade back in. Nearly two days later. He is alive and has a good chance of recovery (in fact, he does make a strong recovery and return to his normal life pattern).

Tell us what was it like? What did you experience?

"Experience? Not a thing! They tell me that my heart stopped, and it took a long time for it to get going again. I guess that means I was dead. Dead! But you couldn't prove it by me. I don't remember a thing, not from the time I spoke to the nurse until I saw my wife standing over me, and then I realized I was in a hospital."

What? No out-of-body experience? No passage through a long, dark tunnel? No sense of euphoria? No magnificently mystical experience? "Not a thing. I just slipped away, faded out—and then slipped back in again. What happened in between, I only know from what people told me. Say, Doc . . . I haven't disappointed you, have I? But that's how it was."

## The New "Life After" Literature

This vignette must seem like a letdown, an anecdote without a punch line, a story not worth the telling. In the supercharged atmosphere of today's fantasy market, the reentry trip, the coming back down to earth, can be disappointing. The fun is over. But we all may be better off if we start to prepare for the descent from the giddy heights of uncritical thought. If history is any teacher, then the current fascination with "life after life" will give way as some new mind trip arises to take its place—and as it encounters some hard knocks against reality. But in the meantime there is the potential for real pain, real suffering, real errors in judgment that increase the jeopardy of ourselves and our loved ones. The fantastic voyage may not be worth its price in actual suffering.

The current wave of interest has two related sources. Elisabeth Kübler-Ross, a charismatic lecturer on the care of the dying person, has been asserting that she has conclusive evidence for survival of bodily death. Her remarks to both lay and professional audiences were quickly picked up by the media. While these assertions might have received little notice if made by an obscure person, Kübler-Ross is in all probability the best-known figure in the emerging field of concern that is known, for want of a better term, as thanatology ("the study of death"). Her books, especially *On Death and Dying* (1969), have been widely read and influential.

Although Kübler-Ross has not yet shared her material on this subject in detail, she contributed an enthusiastic foreword to Raymond A. Moody, Jr.'s book *Life After Life* (1975). This "stamp of approval," carrying much weight because of her reputation, actually goes beyond what Moody claimed for his contribution. Kübler-Ross states that

> it is research like Dr. Moody presents in his book that will enlighten many and will confirm what we have been taught for 2,000 years—that there is life after death. Though he does not claim to have studied death itself, it is evident from his findings that the dying patient continues to have a conscious awareness of his environment after being pronounced clinically dead. This very much coincides with my own research, which has used the accounts of patients who have died and made a comeback, totally against our expectations and often to the surprise of . . . physicians.

The core of Moody's presentation is based upon his interviews with fifty people who either had been pronounced clinically dead by their physicians or had come close to death—and who survived to tell the tale. He detected fifteen separate elements among their reports that occurred frequently. From these commonalities he con-

structed a typical or "ideal" experience. Moody points out that nobody actually reported all these elements as part of the same experience and that there were individual variances in the configuration
and sequence of the components. Nevertheless, some central features emerged.

The "typical" report involves a dying person who hears a physician pronounce him dead. A loud and uncomfortable noise sur-
rounds him, and he has a sense of moving through a long, dark
tunnel. There is a sudden discovery that he is outside of his body,
observing the immediate physical scene as though a spectator. It
takes a while to adjust to this fantastic new condition. Soon, Moody
describes,

> he glimpses the spirits of relatives and friends who have already died,
> and a loving, warm spirit of a kind he has never encountered before—a
> being of light—appears before him. This being asks him a question,
> nonverbally, to make him evaluate his life and helps him along by
> showing him a panoramic, instantaneous playback. . . . At some point
> he finds himself approaching some sort of barrier or border, apparently
> representing the limit between earthly life and the next life. Yet, he
> finds that he must go back to the earth, that the time for his death has
> not yet come. At this point he resists, for by now he is taken up with his
> experiences in the afterlife and does not want to return. He is over-
> whelmed by intense feelings of joy, love, and peace.

The double stimulus of Kübler-Ross's public assertions and the
Moody book has triggered a release of similar reports from many
quarters. The basic route from "dead" through "dark tunnel" to
"light" is often recounted. At times there is the sentiment that the
"dead" person did not want resuscitative efforts to be made. It was
so peaceful in the new state of being that there was little or no
motivation to return to ordinary life.

These reports have quickly found their way into Sunday supple-
ments, radio and television talk shows, and a variety of workshops
and lectures across the nation. The serious clinician, researcher, or
educator has a difficult time avoiding the topic lest he or she be
considered out of date. People who hop adroitly from one band-
wagon to the next have had no difficulty in becoming instant experts on the subject and inflicting their wisdom on curious listeners
and readers.

It is for simple, practical reasons—rather than for any impulse to be the wet blanket at an exuberant party—that I introduce a few considerations that are not likely to be popular.

## The Negative Instance

We started with a sort of counteranecdote. The negative instance has always commanded respect from careful observers. It is a safe bet that if Newton had seen just one apple fall *up* from a tree, this negative instance would have led to a different theory of gravitation. Whether in science or daily life, the alert mind acknowledges and even seeks out possible exceptions to the established order of things. At first the flurry of reports about what it is like to die or be dead was itself an exception to usual assumption. For this reason, if for no other, the reports deserved attention. But media-fueled acceleration has rapidly moved ahead of the slower-moving wheels of science and critical scrutiny. That is why it is imperative that we remind ourselves that the negative instance not only exists but is quite abundant.

The heart attack victim already described exemplifies one type of exception: The person who seems to have been knocking at death's door (from one side or the other) and yet has no recollection to offer. But there are some people among us who narrowly survived death and recall the experience clearly but have rather different memories. I remember the clarity and bitterness with which a respected supervisory nurse recalled her own experience as an admission to the emergency room. She was one of four people severely injured in an automobile accident. At the time she was brought into the emergency room, she didn't know the fate of her companions, one of whom was her brother. It was impossible for her to ask anybody—as a matter of fact, she could not utter a sound or move her body. However, like many people in a traumatized state, she could hear the sounds and voices around her.

"This one is gone," a voice was saying. "Let's get to one of the others next." The nurse realized that *she* was the one who had just been dismissed as dead. Her response? "I became furious—just plain furious! No way was I going to stay dead for them!" She

determined to cross the invisible threshold between death and life
(what today we would call social death: The person is regarded by
others as deceased, whatever the biological facts of the situation
might be). Summoning all her willpower, she at last was able to
attract medical attention with slight bodily movements and faint
sounds. "In my mind, I kept shouting 'I'm not dead yet, you bas-
tards!' " I'm not sure if those words came across to them, but some
sounds did get out, and I wouldn't stop talking and moving until I
had convinced them I wasn't DOA."

The experience of this woman was much different from the type
of account offered by Kübler-Ross and Moody. She was "dead
enough" to be taken for a nonsurvivor and passed over during the
critical treatment-or-no-treatment period. Yet she did not float
above the situation, looking down in wonderment and bliss. She
did not protest the efforts made to revive her or feel that a dream of
celestial serenity had been destroyed by overzealous medical per-
sonnel. This woman wanted to live, and she did all in her power to
summon the resources of a severely traumatized body. In retro-
spect, she credits the pronouncement of death as a stimulus for her
recovery. "I've always been good at flying into a fury, and this was
a grand time for it!"

There are still other types of negative instance. People in respira-
tory failure (choking on a bone, seized by an acute episode of em-
physema, undergoing the terror of a massive drug side effect) often
feel as though they are in direct hand-to-hand combat with death.
The battle for breath sometimes is lost temporarily. While consciousness remains, the sense is of urgency and a wish for rescue,
for another life-giving breath. An observer judging by lack of
breath and undetectable pulse might well conclude the person is
dead and gone.

If we turn history back a few pages, then we discover an entire
literature that expresses the dread of premature burial (Kastenbaum
and Aisenberg, 1972). Hundreds of reports describe thousands of
reputed incidents of people taken for dead and either buried
prematurely or narrowly averting this fate. Some of these reports
might be dismissed as erroneous or as fiction (just as some of the
current survival reports might be dismissed). But other reports are
about as "respectable" and well described as one could reasonably

expect. The dread of being taken for dead, in fact, stimulated some of the more bizarre-seeming funeral practices in our recent history; for example, the pull cord placed in the hand of the deceased to permit sounding a bell if he or she "came to" inside the coffin. It also stimulated some of the more macabre pages of fiction. Both the taken-for-true and purely fictional accounts of premature burial kept many an impressionable mind in a state of anxiety.

It is not easy to evaluate the reality basis of these fears of live burial. Epileptic seizures, hysterical swoonings (quite fashionable in our culture for a while), adverse reactions to drugs, and a variety of little-understood physiological reactions to stress and disease seemed to occur with some frequency a few generations ago. The point for us here is that the condition of being dead enough to be treated as deceased by family, friends, and even by physicians was not seen as an enviable, peaceful, blissful state. It was regarded as the most horrible condition the human mind could conceive.

The existence of other types of reports from the dead or almost-dead frontier does not of itself discredit the kind of accounts that make up the current wave of interest. But they do make it difficult to accept the implications, drawn by some, that the process of dying-unto-death is universally a joyous one.

With today's medical technology it is no longer uncommon for a person to enter that ill-defined realm between what most of us are prepared to regard as normal life and "the other side." There are legitimate reasons for disagreement, controversy, and shifting opinions as to where/when/how life ends and death begins. Our thinking is not always clear on this subject. Sometimes we speak of death as though it were an event, a happening that strikes at a particular time. But sometimes we think of death as though it were a state—in effect, death is what happens after death strikes (not an especially helpful pair of ideas). The definition of death is also highly influenced by both what we can do and what we want to do in the situation. This person is dead in the view of Observer A, who does not know of any techniques that might restore life; Observer B, however, knows one more thing that might work and so simply defers the conclusion of death in order to give survival another chance. Two centuries ago this might have been the difference between realizing or not realizing that an apparently drowned person might be revived by mouth-to-mouth resuscitation. Today it might be the difference in knowledge of heart massage or diabetic coma. The desire to make an all-out effort to bring a person back from apparent death is also variable. We are more willing to abandon life-saving efforts for some people than for others, whether we are speaking of critical moments in an obvious life-or-death situation or the differential pattern of opportunity and care our society makes available over a person's total life span.

Among even the most informed individuals and those most interested in maintaining or restoring life, however, there is room for disagreement on the "deadness" of the victim and the value of resuscitative procedures. And we simply do not know if those who return with happily-ever-after dreams rudely interrupted by medical intervention were more or less dead than those who were struggling with every ounce of strength to come back and those who don't remember a thing.

The media have lavished selective attention on those instances in which a person returns from a trip to the life-death borderline with a comforting, even enviable, tale to tell. In my opinion these tales are certainly worth the telling and the listening. Who could have so little curiosity as to ignore such a rich vein of human experience? And who could be so cynical as to deny the intriguing consistencies, the patterns of agreement among many of the reported experiences (the completely different patterns of negative instance not withstanding)? Certainly, let us share and mull over such experiences.

But let us also admit that we have no satisfactory information on the frequency of such experiences as stacked up against all the encounters that take place in the life-death border territory.* Some people have come to the hasty conclusion that dying and/or being dead fits tidily into the pattern of accounts reported in such books as Moody's (this, by the way, is not a conclusion that Moody himself urges upon us). Were this conclusion entitled to status as a universal law—really telling us what death is—then there should be no negative instances. None. But the apples keep falling up from the tree. Negative instances can be collected by the bushel. It just happens that there is no market for them.

---

*But see Garfield, chapter 4, for a first sampling of statistics on this question.

## Unanswered Questions

Research questions exist at every turn. For example, what kinds of people afflicted with what types of life-threatening ailments or traumas and receiving what kinds of treatment for what lengths of time turn out to be positive or negative instances of the happily-ever-after tales? Truly useful information might emerge from a serious research effort, but perhaps something would be lost in popularity for talk shows and the lecture circuit.

Furthermore, it is obvious that we hear only from those who return to our midst. This is perhaps the most distinctive feature of the current round of interest in the afterlife. The sense of being in contact with a dead person through dreams, the intervention of a medium, or some other form has been experienced by many people over the years. This type of phenomenon is worthy of attention, even though many psychologically oriented scientists have found it easy to ignore. But what is relatively new today is the presence of the person himself, the individual who came that close to death or, depending upon our definition, actually dies and now has returned in flesh as well as spirit.

Even if everybody who returned from such an extreme experience had the same basic story to tell, this would not prove that dying is a pleasure and death a state of bliss. We would still have a firm "no comment" from those who stayed dead. The close call or the temporary death may be quite distinct from the one-way passage.

Furthermore, there is a striking resemblance between the typical survival reports that are making the rounds today and experiences that many individuals have had when not threatened with death. So-called mystical experiences, such as those recounted by Thomas Merton (1971), could easily be taken for accounts of a round-trip voyage to death. The fact that many people have come close to death without reporting the "typical" survival experience while other have had similar psychological experiences without the proximity to physical death invites more curiosity and responsible research rather than hasty conclusions.

Other kinds of arguments can be directed against hasty acceptance of the survival reports as indicating anything directly about death or anything in general about the dying process. The reports continue to justify attention, even though it is premature to arrive at firm conclusions. We are a long way from being able to accept reports of out-of-body experiences, blissful dying, and heavenly death as anything other than fascinating psychological (and perhaps psychobiological) phenomena that deserve the best thinking we can bring to them.

## "The Thrill of Dying"

What concerns me most is the effect of indulgent, uncritical thinking. Many of us are still so unnerved by the prospect of dying and death that we grasp at any shield for protection. In the case at hand, anecdotal reports at times have been misrepresented or accepted as though they were scientific evidence.

Much of the problem resides in our hunger for reassurance against both the real and imagined exigencies of dying and death. And the problem is also with those who offer to feed this hunger in a slick "quickie meal" fashion. Consider, for example, one of the new books that is attempting to ride the waves of public interest. In the Reverend Archie Matson's *Afterlife* (1977) there is a chapter devoted to "The Thrill of Dying." The thrill of dying? This term must have a peculiar sound as it echoes in the minds of people who daily work with the terminally ill and with the dying and their families as well. Both the idea of a "thrill" and the Matson book in general inhabit a fantasy world that is far from actual experience. They bear no resemblance to what takes place in intensive care units, in nursing homes, or inside the family constellation where a loved one is oscillating between home and hospital, remission and critical danger. There is no acknowledgment of the bone-aching depletion experienced by nurses and other care givers, by family, by friends, and by the dying person as well. At one point Matson actually informs us that dying is "fun."

This denial of the realities of the dying process, thinly covered with a veneer of religion, is not what chaplains see and experience when they overcome their own human hesitancies to work intimately with the dying. It is not faith, but faith's counterfeit, that is merchandised by such presentations, just as it is not science, but science's caricature, that is offered as evidence. The ordeals that many undergo every day and the complexities of their thoughts and feelings are trivialized by glib assurances of this kind (for example, "Firstly, death is painless and pleasant!").

How long it has taken for society to appreciate both the emotional and physical distress of the terminally ill person! How much effort has gone into promoting a new attitude! How difficult it remains in many situations to ensure that terminal illness does not result in alienation, abandonment, and despair! Just at a moment in our culture's reevaluation of life and death when there is some authentic hope for helping the terminally ill person to live well and meaningfully, just at this moment we are blinded and distracted by beatific visions.

The happily-ever-after theme threatens to draw attention away from the actual situations of the dying persons, their loved ones, and their care givers over the days, weeks, and months preceding death. What happens up to the point of the fabulous transition from life to death recedes into the background. This could not be more unfortunate. The background, after all, is where these people are actually living until death comes. The view that "all's well that ends well" assumes that everybody passes through a definitive moment of death. This is a questionable concept, not very well supported by clinical experience. Forget the famous last words you have read (some of them never actually uttered) or heard voiced in films and television melodramas. In practice, the transition from life to death is not so clear-cut. It is not so easy to say precisely when life passes into death. Furthermore, the states of consciousness around the time of death can vary widely. Some people are tuned into the world around them and think and speak lucidly until virtually the last breath. Others are comatose for long periods of time. Still others move in and out of contact or show an altered state of consciousness that is neither entirely "in" nor entirely "out."

Strong emphasis on the moment the soul is assumed to depart the body (or the projection of the psyche into a higher plane, if you prefer) might be justified from the perspective of the theologian or the dramatist. But in practice it can lead to a misdirection of attention. Terminally ill people have many human needs, some of them quite simple but nonetheless significant needs that deserve to be met through all the moments that are still left to them. These include such physical needs as relief of thirst; relief from an uncomfortable position; relief from pain and other symptoms that undermine their ability to think clearly, maintain a sense of self-control, or prepare themselves to die as they would prefer.

Through the years there have always been some physicians, nurses, and lay people who have been sensitive to these needs. They have done their best to help terminally ill persons remain themselves until the end. Their good examples have preserved a precious tradition of care and comfort during the long period of our society's neglect of the terminally ill. Today the concept of "death with dignity" is familiar, although subject to sloganeering and misinterpretation. However, the general commitment of the health-care system and our society in general to recognize and provide what the dying person needs has not yet become solidly established. What an unfortunate time to steal attention away from what can be done by dedicated, day-by-day care and bemuse ourselves instead with fantasies about the moment of death and the assumed pleasure that follows!

The psychological and social needs of the terminally ill person are no less real than the physical (even if these different types of need could be neatly separated from one another: They cannot). One person, for example, has a strong need to complete some tasks and obligations before death intervenes. Another person cannot have his or her mind at ease until taking leave of loved ones in a way that will satisfy him or her. The particular constellations of needs are as varied as the people themselves—and since everybody dies, this could hardly be more varied. But attention to the individual needs of terminally ill people (and to the family and friends who virtually live and die with them) is distracted by indulgent visions of the happily ever after. Many a terminally ill person and his or her most important people need the remaining time to share thoughts and feelings and to prepare for what is to come. It may be a comforting thought that the end itself will be a kind of liberation, free from emotional or physical pain. In this regard the survival accounts may have a useful contribution to make.

Yet there is still the very special human dilemma to contend with: not enough and too much time at the same time. There may not be enough time to do (or undo) all that the dying person and his or her loved ones would prefer, and there may be too much time to grow weary and depleted. Life before death counts, too.

## Ending It All

Stories about "the thrill of dying" and the bliss of death threaten the living in another way. Some large but unknown number of people—young and old, in all walks of life—go through periods when life no longer seems worth the living. The individual is tempted to get away, to end it all. This might take the form of suicide or of reckless, self-destructive actions that increase the probability of premature death. Some people follow through on this impulse. Fortunately, however, many of us find alternative solutions. Death tempts; we waver but do not succumb.

One of the barriers to suicide and other forms of premature death is death itself—or, rather, the mental prospect of death. Do we really want to trade familiar disappointments, frustrations, and pains for a step into the void? We draw back, gather our strength, and seek less radical solutions. Even so, death has not been quite the barrier that it might be to suicide in our society. In our tradition it is all too easy to fuzz the distinction between, say, death and sleep, death and a nice long rest, death and a pleasant journey to parts unknown. Impressionable minds (children, people caught up in seemingly unsolvable dilemmas, the sick and weary, the rejected and dejected) may uncritically accept an outlook that our society has held in front of them all their lives. Death seems to be less demanding, perhaps more friendly, than life—and not as different from life as the cold sober mind would probably acknowledge.

This tendency to imagine death as less than death often reveals itself in the thoughts of suicidal people. These individuals sometimes see themselves in a sort of split-screen consciousness: They are dead, the act of suicide has been completed, but there they are, looking down at the results and noting with a sense of achievement what their act accomplished. This is perhaps a variant of the out-of-body experience. It takes place before the fact and makes it that much easier to proceed with self-annihilation.

This tendency is seen also in suicides or ambiguous deaths (mixtures of suicide, accident, illness, miscalculation) that involve drugs. When we need that extra good night's sleep, or when our mood is too "up" or too "down," it is an accepted, commercially lucrative practice to turn to the pill. When death is seen as something less than death, merely as a really good escape from what ails us, then the risk of suicide increases.

From this standpoint the vision of death as a euphoric trip markedly increases the hazard to life. Why resist? Why seek for alternatives? Death is a happier state than any we know on earth, and the passage, the dying process, is itself a most pleasant interlude.

Centuries ago the Catholic church established a firm policy against suicide. The theological case was made by no less than St. Augustine and reaffirmed and strengthened by no less than St. Thomas Aquinas. Other thinkers, not necessarily Catholic, arrived at the same conclusion based upon philosophical argument. Yet there was also a clear practical reason for the early Christian theologians to seek a countervailing force against suicide: Martyrdom was just too appealing, too popular. Glorious death through suffering exerted a hold on too many minds.

Today it is a gratifying image of death-minus-the-suffering that is engendered by the current wave of survival accounts. People who might otherwise have stayed their hands, found alternative solutions, and gone on to fulfilling lives in human society will become suicide statistics or numbered among those who rushed into death by other modalities. I do not believe the frustrated adolescent, the unemployed worker, the grieving widow, or the ailing old person needs to be offered the invitation to suicide on quite so glittering a silver platter.

## References

Kübler-Ross, E., *On Death and Dying*. New York: Macmillan, 1969.

Kastenbaum, R., and Aisenberg, R. B., *The Psychology of Death*. New York: Springer, 1972.

Matson, A., *Afterlife*. New York: Harper & Row, 1977.

Merton, T., *Contemplative Prayer*. Garden City: Doubleday Image, 1971.

Moody, R., Jr., *Life After Life*. Covington, Ga.: Mockingbird Books, 1975.

# 3

# The Same Old Story:
# A Historical Perspective

*Barbara Ross*

*Humankind's curiosity about death did not wait until science pro-
claimed itself established. This is just as well, since some of the core
questions have not yet yielded themselves to controlled empirical inquiry and perhaps never will.*

*Barbara Ross, a psychologist with special interest in the history of her
field and of science in general, guides us on a journey from* The Book of
the Dead *through the formative days of science and to the threshold of
current work on psi phenomena, including the possibility of communication between living and dead. Particular attention is given to the observations of F. H. W. Myers, William James, and Gardner Murphy.*

*It becomes clear that scholars, scientists, and psychologists have been
grappling for a long time with problems that are still with us today,
although in somewhat different forms. There may be much to learn from
their observations. How many minds do we have today that are superior
to Myers's, James's, and Murphy's? Better knowledge of our history
of inquiry into possible communication between living and dead might at
the least enable us to proceed more quickly through our own cycle of
errors and might even provide crucial keys to further understanding.*

Looking behind the pages of official history, one finds a general
public of millions who have transmitted the traditions and practices
of the occult from generation to generation. These traditions and

practices include belief in life after death and communication with the dead. However, considering the long-standing reluctance of science to deal with these possibilities, it is striking that scientists in the twentieth century are discussing the topic in formal meetings and publications. Perhaps such concerns are cyclical. Well over a century ago many intellectuals and scientists thought it strange that so little had been done in *their* modern day to grasp or criticize such notions.[1] They attempted, against many difficulties, to settle the questions once and for all. After thirty years of grappling with the questions, one nineteenth-century researcher concluded that his study "simply brings us back to the creeds of the Stone Age. We have come round again to the primitive practices of the shaman and the medicine-man, to a doctrine of spiritual intercourse which was once universal, but has now taken refuge in African swamps and Siberian tundras and the snow-clad wastes of the Red Indian and Esquimaux."[2] This "doctrine of spiritual intercourse," held in many forms by a variety of minds worldwide through the centuries, provides no easy access for the scientific temperament. As H. G. Wells said, "The human mind is a necessary factor in these experiments and they demand concessions and limiting conditions known in no other field of research."[3]

Today no one can prove conclusively that life after death either does or does not exist. Elisabeth Kübler-Ross suggests that ongoing research "will confirm what we have been taught for two thousand years—that there is life after death." To gain this confirmation, "we have to have the courage to open new doors and admit that our present-day scientific tools are inadequate for many of these new investigations."[4] But despite the new upsurge of research, the factual truth seems to grow closer only to become more elusive. Do our new data provide new significance, or are we simply uncovering contemporary examples of ancient phenomena?

## Life-Death Beliefs in Ancient Times

An early source, *The Book of the Dead* (based on an analysis of the Theban Recension of the Book of the Dead), reveals that during the Dynastic Period the Egyptian expected after death to enter the Judgment Hall of Osiris and believed implicitly that he would there begin an everlasting life in felicity.[5] In order to do his will on earth, moreover, Osiris, was empowered to return the dead to life.[6] Ceremonies represented in the *Book of the Dead* demonstrate that the deceased regains his memory, speech, and physical movements. The restoration of the heart was crucial in this process, for the heart was one of the two foci of the Egyptian dual soul. Once the heart was restored to the body, the heart-soul of the deceased was free to leave the body at the gates of the Other World.[7] Some ceremonies allowed the deceased to make any transformation he pleased—for example, to a crocodile or other animal—and return to earth.[8] The *Book of the Dead,* which contains material gathered from every part of Egypt and the Sudan, reveals beliefs in the resurrection of a spiritual body, recognition of relatives and friends after death, and the continued existence of the heart-soul. All these tenets exist in similar forms today among most of the religious tribes of the Sudan.[9]

In Greece Plato and Aristotle believed that sleep and dreaming were perhaps related to psychic powers beyond physical laws; Democritus was aware that the mind might perceive independently of the senses. The ecclesiastical writings of the Christian Era included many accounts of communication with the dead, apparitions, levitation, and other paranormal events. Accounts by St. Joseph and Augustine are classic examples, but there are hundreds of others.[10]

## The Scientific Revolution

As advancing technology brought improved means of travel and communication, the accepted bases of truth—the Scriptures and scholastic sources—came under closer scrutiny. Some intellectuals decided that determination of truth should be based on organized and definite observation. This threat to Scholasticism led to the Scientific Revolution in the seventeenth century, as mounting evidence opposed the long-accepted standards. A small group, with Francis Bacon as its patron, founded the Royal Society of London. They raised new questions and established methods based on observation rather than faith, intended to reassess man's place in the universe and facilitate the development of valid standards. This was the beginning of modern science. These "new philosophers," our early scientists, vowed to handle only questions of natural philosophy, avoiding theological or supernatural issues. Nevertheless, they published numerous discourses dealing with unusual phenomena. The first major scientific journal, *Proceedings* (begun in 1665), published articles by Descartes and Leibnitz: Among others, they felt compelled to reconcile old issues with the revolutionary approach. Research was directed toward the discovery of natural explanations for phenomena formerly considered totally outside the realm of natural science. Joseph Glanvill, an active member of the Royal Society, critically investigated reports of hauntings.[11] Despite good effort and organization, his investigations failed to determine the facts, and by the end of the seventeenth century questions that were outside the realms of natural law and direct observation fell out of fashion with the scientists.[12]

## The Impact of Mesmerism

In the middle of the eighteenth century, however, the widespread popularity of mesmerism challenged science to once again study the paranormal. Hypnosis, clairvoyance, telepathy, and communication with the dead were examined by commissions formed to sift through the facts and possibly expose fraud. Hundreds of papers debated the issues,[13] and the controversy continued in public and scientific circles.

In the nineteenth century, hypnotism as studied by Janet, Charcot, and other medical people became accepted by some scientists, while others were reluctant to support it because it developed from mesmerism. Although most reports never suggested evidence of ESP (extrasensory perception), it is clear that mesmerism brought the study of paranormal phenomena within the range of serious science. The two major positions were those of: (1) the doctors and scientists, who believed that *suggestion* was the cause of altered consciousness states; and (2) the occultists, who, like Mesmer, posited new psychic fluids through which experience and sensation could pass from one mind to another. Spiritualism, which competed with medical hypnosis, caught on because of the impersonal nature of science and evolutionary biology.[14] "Scientific religion" caught the American public's fancy and added great momentum to psychical research, largely through the influence of Emanuel Swedenborg, a former scientist and philosopher who demonstrated clairvoyance and wrote several books about his communication with the dead. The basic tenet of Spiritualism was that the dead may influence and contact the living through some form of ESP. Many factors helped to set the mood for the popularity of Spiritualism. Science had become less dogmatic; materialism had declined because of Darwin's work; Newtonian mechanics had suffered drastic changes; and Christian Science as well as phrenology were in blossom. The Fox sisters in Hydesville, New York were famous proponents of the movement. Their reputed contact with the dead brought them wide fame and they lectured throughout the United States. Despite many examinations, their claims were never clearly proven to be fraudulent.

Mind-cure, mental healing, and Adventism represented and raised questions of vast importance to the general public. They offered consolation through belief in man's supernatural resources. The human mind and its powers were little understood, and psychic phenomena could not be discounted just because they conflicted with known principles of science. William James considered the question of communication with the dead as reasonable as any other question. Academic psychologists, medical people, and scientists in general denounced Spiritualism. However, James referred to these scientists "from [Hugo] Munsterberg up, or down" as "insufficient authorities." He wrote, "Their interests are most incomplete and their professional conceit and bigotry immense." As for physicians, with their airs of superiority, they "had no more science in them than a fox terrier."[15]

During James's time, paranormal phenomena offered worlds wider than physics could offer and suggested that our natural experience was but a fragment of the possibilities of human experience. But just as the growth of Spiritualism was influenced by psychological and sociological conditions, so was its decline. Because of political factors and the exposure of the fraud of many prominent mediums, as a formal movement Spiritualism failed in the United

States. It left behind several well-established, independent reli-
gions—Christian Science is one example—that, however, did not
hold with communication with the dead.


## Investigations of Paranormal Phenomena

In England Spiritualism gained attention through the work of Sir
William Crookes, a chemist. Crookes set out to expose the entire
Spiritualist movement as fraudulent, but his experiments supported
paranormal phenomena, including communication with the dead.
When he published his results in the *Quarterly Journal of Science* in
1874, his colleagues tried to undercut his credibility, despite his
fine reputation as a scientist.

Although many published reports were questionable, others
strongly suggested psi phenomena: spirit writing, trancelike states,
trance speaking, clairvoyance, spiritual impersonation, spirit music, apparitions, and possession. As public and scientific interest
grew, commissions were set up to investigate testimony. In 1869
the London Dialectical Society experimentally produced telekinetic
effects, and their published report in 1871 supported the genuine-
ness of the phenomena. Alfred Russell Wallace and other eminent
scientists accepted the creed of the Spiritualist movement and lent
the dignity needed to establish well-organized scientific psychical
research.[16]

As more and more scientists became interested, it was clear that
some kind of formal establishment had to be created to handle the
controversial issues surrounding psychic phenomena. In 1882 the
Society for Psychical Research (SPR) was founded. Early members
included Professors Sidgwick and Myers of Cambridge University,
Edmund Gurney, and other scientists of various disciplines who
contributed to the Society's journal, *Proceedings*. Some Spiritualist
leaders who were interested in scientific analysis also were members. During this time, when the SPR was concerned with publishing "hard-headed" articles, James believed that the Society's journal "demonstrated the most hard-headedness and never-sleeping
suspicion of sources of error."[17]

The purpose of the Society for Psychical Research was two-fold:

(1) to carry on systematic experimentation with hypnotic subjects, mediums, clairvoyants, and others; and (2) to collect evidence concerning apparitions, haunted houses, and similar phenomena that were incidentally reported but that "from their fugitive character, admit of no deliberate control."[18] The SPR was a highly disciplined group determined to settle matters once and for all using accepted scientific methods that included specific criteria of evidence and experimental programs. Before the universities became involved, the SPR was the nucleus for parapsychological research and dealt largely with the main tenet of Spiritualism—the belief that psi phenomena indicated some form of survival after death. Most prominent psychics claimed that their impressions came from the deceased, so the Society examined evidence concerning telepathic impacts of dying persons. Hundreds of cases were scrutinized by the SPR and each was given a credulity rating.

It seems appropriate to ask why so many people spent so much time thinking about the paranormal. Why were these problems important, and how were they handled? F. W. H. Myers of Cambridge suggested that evidence for a spirit world had to be continuous with evidence based on our experience in a world of matter and continuous with known fact. Until the nineteenth century this attitude was not part of the development of psychic research: Explanations had been sought outside natural law. Myers and his colleagues believed that all cognizable mind was as continuous as all cognizable matter. They agreed that in popular parlance they were looking for ghosts, but they first wanted to indicate the manifest errors of the traditional view and remove the unfounded theories and explanations of earlier times.[19] They hoped to collect enough concrete facts to eventually theorize beyond the established nonscientific explanations that were no longer satisfactory.

Myers and his colleagues pursued data that appeared to suggest a more central place for man in a seemingly deterministic universe. A central question to Myers was: "Is the Universe friendly?"[20] If the existence of life after death could be proved, he thought: (1) we would take a large step in our understanding of the universe; (2) the knowledge of life in man independent of blood and brain would dominate and change all science and philosophy; and (3) the application of this new knowledge could open limitless prospects for further knowledge. Although Myers never claimed that the discovery had been made, he hoped that the evidence available would demonstrate that the ancient problem could be realistically attacked. He made clear his own belief in the imminent possibility of proof, saying that "it benefits all men of good will to help toward this knowing."[21] Myers's major goal was to show that the depths of human personality disclose indications of life and faculty not limited to a planetary existence or to this material world. He promoted the belief that these indications pointed to a spiritual world "inhabited" in some way by the dead.

In the early years of the SPR the emphasis was on information collection rather than on experimental research. This collection of individual cases was *Phantasms of the Living*, written by Edmund Gurney, Frank Podmore, and Myers. Their most difficult challenge was to soundly evaluate the compiled reports of personal experiences. They considered ordinary testimony almost worthless in its support of psi phenomena. Despite the SPR's efforts to solidify their evidence, the public press criticized their work when it was published in 1886. Nevertheless, the SPR had compiled a collection that was large enough to exhibit certain patterns and principles of psi phenomena as experienced in daily life. Many researchers shifted their focus from the study of professional psychics to people in general. They thought that *everyone* might have potential for psychic experiences, not just a selected few. With more and more cases being reported, definite psi categories clarified themselves, and occurrences were well beyond chance or coincidence.

In 1894 another extensive study was published: *The Census of Hallucinations*. This survey attempted to determine whether individuals who believed themselves completely awake had experienced sensory impressions of voices, objects, or beings that had no apparent external source. The analysis of 25,000 reported occurrences made a significant addition to the work begun by *Phantasms of the Living* and provided information for further consideration of the rapidly growing question.

Various interpretations appeared, including the suggestion that even psychoses might be evolutionary and representative of an effort toward self-development, self-adaptation, or self-renewal.[22] Gurney's work with hypnotic automatic writing influenced Janet's effort, which in turn provided some of the first stepping-stones toward a comprehension of multiple personalities. During the last twenty years of the nineteenth century, Myer's developing theory of a subliminal level of cognition began gathering support and experimental evidence through the work of Von Hartmann, Charcot, and Janet.[23]

In 1900 Professor Theodore Flournoy of the University of Geneva noted the remarkable progress of psychology during the previous twenty years, particularly in the realization of complex continuous thoughts and feelings below the threshold of consciousness. Flournoy saw no reason to consider mediumship pathological, despite its rareness, and he suggested that if telepathy did not exist we would have to invent it. Liébeault of the "Nancy School" published examples of telepathic impulses proceeding directly from a dying person, although Myers ascribed these impulses to the action of the spirit after bodily death.[24]

Psychical researchers were no longer obligated to justify their belief in a correlation between deaths and crisis apparitions. It was up to critics to explain away the accumulated evidence. In the final analysis Myers was convinced that his theory presented evidence of man's survival after death. Like many of today's researchers, he interviewed people who were dying or awakening from coma,[25] and his in-depth reports appeared in *Proceedings* and in medical and surgical journals as early as 1889. He noted inarticulate sounds from or near the patients and thought that perhaps these sounds were messages of welcome to the dying. No cases of posthumous intelligence implied discomfort or wickedness; all seemed to be indications of love toward living persons.

William James concluded that: (1) the spirit holds contact with a living man, located in a certain place at a certain moment, and animated by certain thoughts and emotions; (2) the spirit can in some cases find and follow the man as it pleases and is cognizant of our space and time as well as of certain aspects of our past and future; (3) the spirit is partly conscious of the thought and emotions of its earthly friend, not only when the friend is in the presence of the "sensitive,"* but also when the friend is at home and living his

*The "sensitive" is a person who is thought to be unusually receptive to paranormal messages.

ordinary life; and (4) the spirit has occasional glimpses of material fact upon the earth, not manifestly proceeding through any living mind.[26]

How would the spirit attempt to communicate with the living? If we consider earlier accounts such as those of the Egyptians, it seems likely that the spirit might want to communicate with the living if it retains not only memory of earthly loves but also fresh consciousness of loving emotion towards it after death. Myers thought the spirit might seek as an avenue something like light, a glimmer of translucency in the material world. This light could indicate the presence of a human organism so constituted that a spirit could temporarily inform or control it. Interestingly, today's research has encountered conceptions of images similar to those of Myers.

Gardner Murphy wrote that Myers was aware of late-nineteenth-century developments in medicine, psychology, and psychiatry, as well as in the psychical field, and praised his courage in studying an area unaccepted by the science of the day.[27] Aldous Huxley thought it strange that Myers's "amazingly rich, profound, and stimulating book should have been neglected in favor of descriptions of human nature less complete and of explanations less adequate to the given facts."[28] Huxley considered Myers's account of the unconscious superior to Freud's because it was more comprehensive and truer to the data of experience and superior to Jung's because of its foundation on concrete facts. Myers was neither a doctor nor a trained psychologist and had no vested interest in sickness. Huxley appreciated him as "a classical scholar, a minor poet, a conscientious observer, and a platonic philosopher; therefore he was free to pay more attention to the positive aspects of the subliminal self than to the negative and destructive aspects."[29]

Although for half a century psychologists had fully admitted the existence of a subliminal mental region, they had never systematically explored the extent of the region or sought to determine its boundaries. Myers devotedly attacked these unknowns, and his speculations were the first attempt in any language to consider the phenomena of hallucinations, hypnotism, automatism, double personality, and mediumship as connected parts of a whole subject. William James considered Myers's attempt to organize paranormal phenomena into classes and series as the first great step toward overcoming the distaste of orthodox science for these subjects.[30]

In 1885 an American branch of the Society for Psychical Research was formed. Later it joined forces with the British society. James served as the major American representative and spent a considerable part of his life examining psychic phenomena. He willingly took the part of the vigorous scientific disbeliever, but shared deep intellectual sympathy with Myers. Despite his denouncement of late-nineteenth-century experimental psychology, James's evaluation of evidence was always directed by sound scientific sense. Because of their rigid scientific attitudes, reputable American psychologists avoided the psychical research movement, and James almost singlehandedly promoted the cause, as he did later with the psychoanalytic movement.

James complained that psychology had assumed the physical science model and then had refused to consider any alternatives. Scientists denied the significance of paranormal evidence despite the extremely objective attempts of the researchers. James believed that the Society for Psychical Research had restored continuity to history by offering reasonable bases for beliefs formerly considered superstitions and by attempting to bridge the gap between science as an empirical method and studies of interest to humans.[31]

James hoped to convince the scientific community that the scientific method should be applied to questions of general, everyday importance. He was upset that phenomena unclassifiable within the system were labeled "paradoxical absurdities." In his words: "If there is anything which human history demonstrates, it is the extreme slowness with which the ordinary academic and critical mind acknowledges facts to exist which present themselves as wild facts, with no stall or pigeonhole, or as facts which threaten to break up the accepted system."[32] One can easily see how Thomas Kuhn's conception of developments in the history of science is related to James's ideas. James wrote: "Only the born geniuses let themselves be worried and fascinated by . . . outstanding exceptions. . . ."[33] Both men suggested that science will be renovated only by those who will steadily look after regularly irregular phenomena.

As early as 1873 James concluded that not all mental disorders need have a physical basis, that the mind sometimes acts independently of material coercion. He studied the whole realm of psychical research, editing and reporting long series of communications purported to have come from the deceased.[34] He concluded that some external will to communicate probably existed. Myers was more certain, believing that the facts proved: (1) the persistence of the spirit as a structural law of the universe, and the inalienable heritage of each soul; (2) the existence of an avenue of communication between the spiritual and material worlds (traffic on this avenue is the flow of dispatched and received telepathic messages, or the flow of uttered and answered prayers); and (3) the retention in the surviving spirit of some memories and loves of earth.[35]

Why did these scientists deal so seriously with the possibility of life after death? They believed that if science could bridge the gulf between living and discarnate spirits, then better knowledge of the workings of the brain and nervous system might lead to fuller, more coherent communications with the spirit world and to a higher level of unitary consciousness.

In James's time scientists were amazed that a universe which had once seemed so small and simple could be "so vast and mysterious a complication."[36] By 1896 the thoughts of Descartes, Newton, Lyell, Faraday, and James Mill appeared almost childish or innocent. Would the science of James's day appear shallow and narrow to future scientists because of its belief in a strictly impersonal world?

James repeatedly attacked the unwillingness of science to consider the public's beliefs and opinions. He said: "The current of thought in academic circles runs against me, and I feel like a man who must set his back against an open door quickly if he does not wish to see it closed and locked. In spite of its being so shocking to the reigning intellectual tastes, I believe that a candid consideration of piecemeal supernaturalism and a complete discussion of all its metaphysical bearings will show it to be the hypothesis by which the largest number of legitimate requirements are met."[37] James was so impressed by the results of paranormal research that he adopted the hypothesis they so naturally suggested to him: that transmundane energies (God, if you will) produce immediate effects within the natural world to which the rest of our experience belongs.[38]

Although telepathy and communication with or through some higher power were realities to James, he apparently never reached a certainty about survival after death. In 1898 he published a book on human immortality in which he suggested that perhaps the brain acts as a transmitter rather than as an originator of mental processes, so that the deceased may be able to carry on a transphysical existence.[39] Years before James, and without knowledge of the idea of the split personality, a German physicist, Theodor Fechner, arrived at a similar conclusion concerning the possibility of a superior coconsciousness.[40] Given the theoretical explanations of both men, there was no need to posit immortality, as did Myers, although James believed that the facts pointed toward a union with something larger than our conscious selves, in which union we would find our greatest peace. Any larger entity would do; it need not be infinite and might be only a larger and more godlike self, of which the present self is but the partial expression. These are speculations, subject to individual interpretation, but they are important speculations because they occur in some form in almost everyone. Each of us understands the universe only in relation to the self. If the self ceases to exist, where does that leave us? We want to believe that individual character has permanence. This desire contributed to the popularity of Lamarckism, which professed that if an individual had a particular ability, that ability would be genetically passed to the individual's offspring. Of course, the later discovery of chromosomes radically changed opinion about Lamarck's theory, but even in the late twentieth century some people believe his claims.

The work of the British and American Societies for Psychical Research became a major force in world parapsychology as years of investigation provided a vast accumulation of scientifically acceptable evidence for ESP. These societies developed techniques and established criteria for evaluation that are the basis for today's research.

In 1912 a project in psychical research was undertaken at Stanford and later also at Harvard through a William James endowment. Controlled experiments in telepathy were conducted in the 1920s in Holland with an apparatus similar to a galvanometer to determine whether or not the participant was in a passive state of awareness. This research was highly successful and thus the quantitative approach demonstrated that it could uncover evidence for the governing principles of psi phenomena.

Psychical research in the early years was both experimental and descriptive; neither approach could gain acceptance over the other. For decades the difference of opinion continued, and as recently as 1962, a major source, the *Journal of Parapsychology* questioned leading researchers regarding the future directions of research. Some thought it had to be an experimental science, while others believed they had enough quantitative evidence to prove the existence of psi phenomena. The latter suggested a focus on qualitative aspects and the use of insight. Generally, it was felt that parapsychological research was a combination of naturalistic observation and experimental confirmation.

J. B. Rhine proposed that while quantitative work is important in evaluating certain phenomena, quantitative techniques such as statistical analysis should not be the only criterion to establish validity; that is, spontaneous cases need not be subjected to statistical analysis to be valid. Dr. Rhine early defined his boundaries of psychical research to include the study of mediumship, but he shifted parapsychology's emphasis to games of chance, although this had been done before in thought transference studies that were published in *Nature*.

Interest in psi phenomena spread to India, Russia, Italy, Germany, and South America, and psi phenomena eventually became the subject of nearly worldwide attention. Hundreds of painstaking studies are in progress today. As an enlightening investigation into the history of opinions about psi research, it would be interesting to mix examples of century-old research with the latest material. It would be a rare person indeed who could tell them apart. One hundred years ago Myers firmly believed in the imminence of proof for the existence of psi phenomena; today many confidently believe in the same imminence.

William James wrote: "One might say that the savage assumed too little difference between the material and the spiritual world and the philosopher had assumed too much,"[41] while the scientist saw the gulf between the two worlds as unbridgeable. James believed that science and psychology must find a form in which paranormal phenomena can have a positive place. However rare is the capacity for communication between this and the other world, science should attempt to understand and explain it.

# Notes

1. F. W. H. Myers, *Human Personality and Its Survival of Bodily Death*, ed. Susy Smith. New York: University Books, 1961, p. 207.

2. Ibid.

3. H. G. Wells, Julian Huxley, and G. P. Wells, *The Science of Life*. New York: The Book League of America, 1936, p. 1416.

4. Raymond A. Moody, Jr., *Life After Life*. Covington, Ga.: Mockingbird Books, 1975, Introduction.

5. Sir E. A. Wallis Budge, *The Book of the Dead*. 2nd ed., rev. and enl. London: Routledge & Kegan Paul, 1951, Chapters XXX–XXXV.

6. Ibid., Chapter II.

7. Ibid., Chapters XXV–XXVI.

8. Ibid., Chapters LXXVI, LXXXVIII.

9. In the process of transmission, some things were probably altered, misunderstood, or omitted. For examples of why this might have been so, see ibid., pp. CCIII ff. Where the old religious literature wasn't entirely superseded, it must have influenced priests and others in their selection of texts for funerary papyri. The Egyptian masses were intensely conservative and clung to tradition: The older the text, the more they revered it, although they accepted new settings or contexts for old ideas; that is, they were able to reconcile the old with the new. See ibid., pp. CCV ff.

10. For a more detailed treatment, see Moody, *Life After Life*, and D. Scott Rogo, *Parapsychology: A Century of Inquiry*. New York: Dell, 1975.

11. Joseph Glanvill, *Saducismus triumphatus; or full and plain evidence concerning witches and apparitions*. (Originally published 1689.) Gainesville, Fla., 1966.

12. C. R. Weld, *A History of the Royal Society with memoirs of the presidents*. 2 vols. London, 1848, I, 93.

13. Rogo, *Parapsychology*, pp. 40ff.

14. William James, *William James on Psychical Research*, comp. and ed. Gardner Murphy and Robert O. Ballou. New York: Viking, p. 211.

15. James made a speech in 1898 at the State House in Boston in which he opposed a bill regarding licensing of medical practitioners. The bill attempted to abolish faith curers by requiring them to become doctors of medicine. James's speech was published in the *Banner of Light* (March 12, 1898).

16. Rogo, *Parapsychology*.

17. William James, *The Will to Believe, and Other Essays in Popular Philosophy*. London: Longmans, Green, 1897, p. 303.

18. Ibid., p. 304.

19. Myers, *Human Personality*, p. 208.

20. *William James on Psychical Research*, p. 211.

21. Myers, *Human Personality*, p. 262.

22. James, *The Will to Believe*, p. 264.

23. *William James on Psychical Research*, p. 212.

24. Myers, *Human Personality*, pp. 292, 323.

25. Ibid., p. 212.

26. William James, *Human Immortality*. New York: Dover, 1956, p. 400.

27. Myers, *Human Personality*, Introduction.

28. Ibid., p. 7.

29. Ibid., p. 8.

30. James, *The Will to Believe*, p. 316.

31. Ibid., pp. 326ff.

32. Ibid., p. 302.

33. Ibid., p. 300.

34. *William James on Psychical Research*, p. 7.

35. Myers, *Human Personality*, p. 403.

36. James, *The Will to Believe*, p. 327.

37. William James, *The Varieties of Religious Experience: A Study in Human Nature*. London: Longmans, Green, 1903, p. 521.

38. Ibid., p. 198.

39. James, *The Varieties of Religious Experience*, p. 555.

40. Ibid., p. 527.

41. James, *The Will to Believe*, p. 399.

# 4

# The Dying Patient's Concern with "Life After Death"

*Charles A. Garfield*

*What does a psychologist learn from working with people who are fac-
ing a life-threatening disease? Charles A. Garfield, founder of a pio-
neering volunteer counseling service and staff member of a cancer research institute, has had the opportunity to know many terminally ill
individuals. This means he has also had the opportunity to know
people who were experiencing a variety of what are now termed
"altered states of consciousness."*

*From his own clinical and research experience Garfield examines the
current spate of assumptions and conclusions about near-death encounters. He believes that near-death experiences are "a subclass of a
larger group of altered-state experiences attainable through a variety of
techniques and circumstances." Along the way, Garfield offers both
specific information regarding the patient population he has studied and
a general humanistic perspective for viewing such phenomena. Written
on more than one level, this essay calls upon the analytic-thinking and
basic-feeling responses of both author and reader.*

A man is dying and, as he reaches the point of greatest physical distress,
he hears himself pronounced dead by his doctor. He begins to hear an
uncomfortable noise, a loud ringing or buzzing, and at the same time
feels himself moving very rapidly through a long dark tunnel. After this
he suddenly finds himself outside his own physical body, but still in the
immediate physical environment, and he sees his own body from a
distance, as though he is a spectator. He watches the resuscitation at-

Adapted from a paper presented at the 85th Annual Convention of the American
Psychological Association, San Francisco, 1977.

tempt from this unusual vantage point and is in a state of emotional upheaval.

After a while, he collects himself and becomes more accustomed to his odd condition. He notices that he still has a body, but one of a very different nature and with very different powers from the physical body he has left behind. Soon other things begin to happen. Others come to meet and to help him. He glimpses the spirits of relatives and friends who have already died, and a loving, warm spirit of a kind he has never encountered before—a being of light—appears before him. This being asks him a question, nonverbally, to make him evaluate his life, and helps him along by showing him a panoramic, instantaneous play-back of the major events of his life.

At some point he finds himself approaching some sort of barrier or border, apparently representing the limit between earthly life and the next life. Yet, he finds that he must go back to the earth, that the time for his death has not yet come. At this point he resists, for by now he is taken up with his experiences in the afterlife and does not want to return. He is overwhelmed by intense feelings of joy, love, and peace. Despite his attitude, he somehow reunites with his physical body and lives. (Goleman, 1977)[1]

Raymond Moody, Jr., distilled the "normative" near-death experience described above from the 150 anecdotal reports published in his book *Life After Life*. Moody's composite contains the experiences most frequently encountered by people who "had either been resuscitated after being pronounced dead, faced imminent death through injury or illness, or been with individuals who relayed their own experiences as they were dying" (Goleman, 1977). Most fascinating is his observation that these experiences occurred independently of both the individual differences among patients and the events and circumstances that resulted in their brush with death. From his analysis of the data, Moody concluded that the near-death experience profoundly alters a person's consciousness.

Karlis Osis and Erlunder Haraldsson[2] compiled the deathbed observations doctors and nurses in America and India made of nearly 500 dying patients. The most common experience reported by dying patients in both countries was the vision of a human figure. Three out of four patients in this sample had visions of a religious figure or a deceased loved one who came to escort the dying person to another realm.

Elisabeth Kübler-Ross, in collecting as yet unpublished anecdotal reports similar to Moody's, found that many people who had been close to death reported an out-of-body experience; a sensation of elation; an experience of a white light; and an encounter with a luminous being—often a deceased loved one—ready to assist in the transition from life to death. Unlike Moody, who is reluctant to claim that such evidence means survival after physical death, and Osis and Haraldsson, who leave the question open, Kübler-Ross maintains that when people die they transcend the body and proceed to another level of existence (Goleman, 1977). At minimum, Moody's more modest interpretation of near-death experiences and Kübler-Ross's more radical evaluation contribute to a powerful challenge to the materialist paradigm of consensus science.

This chapter will present (1) a brief discussion of the basic paradigmatic clash between the work of Moody, Osis, and others and the prevailing stance of Western science and (2) an analysis of my on-going clinical work with dying cancer patients in which I will compare firsthand clinical experience to the anecdotal reports of Moody, Kübler-Ross, and Osis and Haraldsson.

## The Western Scientific Paradigm

> Each innovator necessitated the community's rejection of one time-honored scientific theory in favor of another incompatible with it. Each produced a consequent shift in the problems available for scientific scrutiny and in the standards by which the profession determined what should count as an admissible problem or as a legitimate problem-solution. And each transformed the scientific imagination in ways that we shall ultimately need to describe as a transformation of the world within which scientific work was done. Such changes, together with the controversies that almost always accompany them, are the defining characteristics of scientific revolutions. (Kuhn, 1962)[3]

One major reason why researchers and clinicians are reluctant to investigate altered states of consciousness (ASC) is the misconception that such inquiry might transgress the current methodology of scientific inquiry. However, a foray into the nature of scientific paradigms and formal logic will not only demonstrate that the foundations for such research already exist but will also explain the necessity for experimentation based on a newly evolving model of scientific inquiry.

What are the philosophical and logical bases of inquiry into altered states of consciousness? Before proceeding into a new area of research, clinicians and theoreticians would do well to examine their own sources, biases, assumptions, and influences from other disciplines. Such an examination would help to insure that the ensuing theory and research is well rooted and broadly based. Establishing the links between the philosophy of science, formal logic, and research in altered states of consciousness is therefore a means of both grounding the new research and transmitting its implications to related disciplines.

According to Kuhn, a paradigm is a "supertheory," or a theoretical formulation of a wide diversity of data into an internally consistent and coherent body of knowledge. Researchers who are philosophically predisposed to accept a paradigm will direct and interpret their scientific activity within its confines. Unfortunately, the rigidity of a paradigm increases as the supertheory becomes an implicit framework for the inclusion and exclusion of certain phenomena. Rather than a tentatively held theory of the structure of the universe, the paradigm becomes dogma, arbitrarily defining the parameters within which researchers must conduct their inquiries. One clear deficiency of a dogma is that it becomes self-perpetuating and thereby self-fulfilling. Alfred N. Whitehead underscores this point in *Science and the Modern World* (1967) when he observes that paradigms impose order upon a basically random order of phenomena. A paradigm serves as a "prism" through which certain phenomena are included for inquiry while others are excluded. The schema directs the attention of researchers to certain groupings and correlations of data that are themselves amenable to that kind of investigation, and the results of that predetermined investigation verify the paradigm. Whitehead points out that the narrow efficiency of the scheme is the very cause of its "supreme methodological success."

For example, Einstein's equations helped initiate the current paradigm of physics, which in turn verifies Einstein's equations. Examples of earlier paradigms are Copernican astronomy, Newtonian physics, and Darwinian evolution. In each case, acceptance of the new paradigm forced the scientific community to reject or radically modify one scientific theory, such as Kepler's astronomy, in favor of another incompatible with it (McCain and Segal, 1969). Each adoption of a new paradigm produces a shift in both the problems acceptable for scientific scrutiny and the definition of what constitutes a valid solution. Furthermore, this shift in perspective transforms the scientific imagination in a manner that can only be described as a profound alteration and transformation of the Weltanschauung of the researcher. Since culture and society are ultimately affected by the prevailing world views of their authorities, be they Nobel-Prize-winning scientists or shamans, the alteration of basic paradigms can have the effect of radically restructuring the world view of all members of a society.

Pervasive alterations in world perspective inevitably meet with resistance even though certain demonstrable phenomena remain inexplicable in terms of the former paradigm. Kuhn explicates the process:

> Novelty emerges only with difficulty, manifested by resistance against a background provided by expectation. Initially, only the anticipated and usual are experienced, even under circumstances where anomaly is later to be observed. The later awareness of anomaly opens a period in which conceptual categories are adjusted until the initially anomalous has become the anticipated. (Kuhn, 1962)

In effect, a paradigm is an agreed-upon set of expectancies that excludes other possibilities. Scientific disciplines are by necessity based on a shared set of expectancies that become manifest in society as the consensual validation of an order of reality. From this consensus people derive their concept of the normality of a certain mode of psychological functioning.

There is great similarity between a paradigm and the concept of a normative state of consciousness. Each is "a complex, interdependent set of rules and theories for interacting with and interpreting experiences within a certain context" (Tart, 1972). In both, the rules and theories have become so implicit that they are no longer recognized as tentative but, instead, operate automatically. Misconceptions concerning the nature of objective inquiry have systematically excluded ASC phenomena as valid subjects for investigation. But we would do well to remember the observation of William James in his *Varieties of Religious Experience:*

Our normal waking consciousness, rational consciousness as we call it, is but one special type of consciousness, whilst all about it, parted from it by the filmiest of screens, there lie potential forms of consciousness entirely different. We may go through life without suspecting their existence; but apply the requisite stimulus, and at a touch they are there in all their completeness, definite types of mentality which probably somewhere have their field of application and adaptation. No account of the universe in its totality can be final which leaves these other forms of consciousness quite disregarded. How to regard them is the question— for they are so discontinuous with ordinary consciousness. Yet they may determine attitudes though they cannot furnish formulas, and open a region though they fail to give a map. At any rate, they forbid a premature closing of our accounts with reality. (James, 1958)

Jung (1961) contends that rationalism and doctrinairism are the disease of our time because they pretend to supply all the answers. His ideas agree with Kuhn's; he believes that "we cannot visualize another world ruled by quite other laws, the reason being that we live in a specific world which has helped to shape our mind and establish our basic psychic condition. We are strictly limited by our innate structure and therefore bound by our whole being and thinking to this world of ours."

He continues with the contention that

A man should be able to say that he has done his best to form a conception of life after death, or to create some image of it—even if he must confess his failure. . . . The more the critical reason dominates, the more impoverished life becomes; but the more of the unconscious, and the more of myth we are capable of making conscious, the more of life we integrate. Over-valued reason has this in common with political absolutism: under its dominion the individual is pauperized.

Hence, "the materialist goes with nothing to cling to into the dark and annihilation."

Bertrand Russell in his *Unpopular Essays* offers the following anecdote: "F. W. H. Myers, whom spiritualism had converted to belief in a future life, questioned a woman who had lately lost her daughter as to what she supposed had become of her soul. The mother replied: 'Oh well, I suppose she is enjoying eternal bliss,

but I wish you wouldn't talk about such unpleasant subjects' . . . "
(Koestler, 1977).

Arthur Koestler notes that Russell's anecdote

> sounds like the perfect paradigm of man's split mind, in which belief
> and disbelief lead an agonized coexistence. The unpleasantness of dying
> is a hard, cold fact. On the other hand, not only eternal bliss (or eternal
> torture), but also the more sophisticated versions of life after death pre-
> sent problems that our minds are incapable of handling: they are far
> beyond the reasoning faculties of our species. (Koestler, 1977)

Freud's own terror of not knowing seems to have resulted in his
conception of Thanatos, the death instinct. His friend and biogra-
pher Ernest Jones offers the following assessment:

> I would say that in the realms of thought and action the distinction
> between men who believe that mental processes or beings can exist
> independently of the physical world, and those who reject this belief, is
> the most significant of all classifications: And I should measure any
> hope of further evolutionary progress by the passage of man from one
> class to another. (Jones, 1959)

More recently, Michael Polanyi and Arthur Koestler have resur-
rected the theory that the higher forms of life are hierarchically
structured in relation to each other. They suggest that although the
view that nothing exists but the physical world may account for
certain levels of consciousness, it may be quite inadequate to describe others. Polanyi (1967) observes that "the hierarchical structure of higher forms of life necessitates the assumption of further
processes of emergence . . . the logical structure of the hierarchy
implies that a higher level can come into existence only through a
process not manifest at lower levels, a process which thus qualifies
as an emergence." Heywood (1968) asks: "Where must those processes stop? Is there any reason why consciousness should not
emerge onto an ultraphysical level of reality where it can exist independently of a physical body?" She concludes with Sir Cyril Burt's
observation: "If modern scientific knowledge affords no evidence
for survival, it is equally true to say that it no longer furnishes any
evidence against it."

## Dying and the Alteration of Consciousness

I just watched my friend die.

> Death is indeed a fearful piece of brutality; there's no sense pretending
> otherwise. It is brutal not only as a physical event, but far more so
> psychically: a human being is torn away from us, and what remains is
> the icy stillness of death. There no longer exists any hope of a relation-
> ship, for all the bridges have been smashed at one blow. (Jung, 1961)

At such times I receive little emotional sustenance from the notion
that death, in the light of eternity, appears as a joyful event, a
wedding, in Jung's terms a "mysterium coniunctionis." My pain is
far more immediate and obvious than my joy whether or not "the
soul attains its missing half and achieves wholeness" (Jung, 1961).
Yet fascination with life after death continues, and for my friend's
sake as well as my own, I openly root for such a possibility.

In my work with the SHANTI Project, a volunteer counseling
service for individuals facing life-threatening illnesses, and at the
Cancer Research Institute at the University of California, San Francisco, I have found that dying patients often experience a combination of powerful ego-annihilating elements: insurmountable contradictions in life situations, extremely severe chemotherapeutic and
radiological toxins, and generally debilitating chemical changes.
Along with Osis (1961), I have observed that altered state experiences reflecting various stages of ego dissolution do occur in the
terminal phases of life. To label these experiences as hallucinatory
and dismiss reports of them as unworthy of consideration or symptomatic of the disease process may be tantamount to ignoring an
invaluable opportunity. If the various Eastern and Western religious traditions and parapsychological disciplines are correct, the
period just before physical death is one of maximal receptivity to
altered state realities (Garfield, 1975). Kastenbaum and Aisenberg
(1972), in reporting the case of a healthy 34-year-old nurse who
nearly died as the result of an unsuspected allergic reaction to peni-
cillin, noted that the final stage in her near-death experience was a
state of bliss symbolized by an image of the Taj Mahal and a profound feeling of being "deeply idyllically engrossed." They continue with the observation that "when the patient began to respond

to resuscitation, she did not want to awaken and was enjoying a markedly wish-fulfilling dream of hypnopompic hallucination which was idiosyncratically appropriate to her affective response to her life situation and took into account the sudden threat to her life" (Kastenbaum and Aisenberg, 1972). Whether we conceptualize this near-death experience in terms of denial, negation, and regression, as did the woman's psychoanalyst, or instead contend that an ego-transcendent experience permitted access to altered state realities every bit as real in their own terms as consensus reality is largely a function of the belief system of the observer. The "letting go, the giving in, the abandonment of striving to maintain object relationships, and the acceptance of passivity is intrinsically a joyous or pleasurable state" (Kastenbaum and Aisenberg, 1972).

I believe it is possible that realistic acceptance of death is for some individuals intimately related to near-death consciousness-altering experiences of a transcendent nature (Garfield, 1977b). About 21 percent of the terminally ill patients I have interviewed had such experiences in the preterminal and/or terminal phases of their illness. Their general reluctance to report these perceptions was directly related to a fear either of being labeled insane or of having their experiences disqualified as hallucinatory. An increased understanding of the dying process, of intense psychic transformation, may require us to acknowledge, along with Laing, that the

ego is the instrument for living in this world. If the ego is fragmented or destroyed (by the insurmountable contradictions of certain situations, by toxins, by chemical changes, etc.), the person experiencing this transformation may be exposed to other worlds, as "real" but different from the more familiar territory of dreams, imagination, perception, and fantasy. (Laing, 1972)

The near-death experiences recorded in the medical and psychological literature are not positive proof of life after death; rather they are altered state experiences not at all specific to the dying process. I have received several letters from women who had very similar experiences during natural childbirth. I believe the near-death experiences described in this chapter are a subclass of a larger group of altered state experiences attainable through a variety of techniques and circumstances.

In the past three years, I have worked with 215 cancer patients who subsequently died. I spent an average of three to four hours a week with them for a period ranging from several weeks to almost two years. Among the 22 percent who told me of their altered state experiences, four groups emerged.

1. One experienced a powerful white light and celestial music (as in Moody's accounts) as well as an encounter (similar to that reported by Osis and Haraldsson) with a religious figure or deceased relative. The patients described these as "incredibly real, peaceful and beautiful."

2. A second experienced demonic figures, nightmarish images of great lucidity.

3. A third reported dreamlike images, sometimes "blissful," sometimes "terrifying," sometimes alternating. The images were not nearly as lucid as those related by the first two groups. However, they appeared to have as great a variation in content.

4. The final groups experienced the Void or a tunnel or both. That is, the patients reported drifting endlessly in outer space or being encapsulated in a limited environment with obvious spatial constraints. A common theme in their accounts was the contrast between maximal freedom and maximal constraint with, in some cases, fluctuation from one to the other.

My work has included interviews with individuals who have had near-death experiences or who have been pronounced clinically dead and then revived. In an effort to evaluate the anecdotal reports of Moody and Kübler-Ross, I conducted in-depth interviews with thirty-six intensive care or coronary care patients. Since my primary function is to provide basic emotional support, I was often the first person to interact with the patient for an appreciable length of time following his brush with death. My contact occurred anywhere from three hours to two days following the incident. Eighteen patients reported no memory of the event at all. Their last memory before losing consciousness was of being in their hospital room and when they awoke they were either in the ICU or CCU "hooked up to the hardware." Seven reported experiences similar to those collected by Moody, Kübler-Ross, and Osis, including seeing a bright light, hearing "celestial" music, and meeting religious figures or deceased relatives. Four reported lucid visions of a demonic or nightmarish nature. Four reported having dreamlike images; in two instances entirely positive and the other two alternating between positive and negative. Three patients reported drifting endlessly in outer space among the planets, but loose as if thrown from a space ship. No significant changes in content were expressed by any of the patients in three interviews conducted at weekly intervals following the event.

In light of this research, three main observations seem important.

1. It appears that not everyone dies a blissful, accepting death. My friend's tortuous, labored breathing during the twenty-four hours before she died hardly appeared blissful. I hope those who suggest that she was really "feeling no pain" thanks to the "immunity" provided by her comatose state or because she was really "out of her body" are correct. However, almost as many of the dying patients I interviewed reported negative visions (encounters with demonic figures, and so forth) as reported blissful experiences, while some reported both.

2. Pelletier and Garfield (1976) note that context is a powerful variable in such altered state experiences as the hypnotic, meditative, psychedelic, schizophrenic. In keeping with the early LSD research, we might very well find that a caring environment including supportive family, friends, and staff is an important factor in maximizing the likelihood of a positive altered state experience for the dying. Certainly, helping dying patients relate to their experiences in a constructive fashion rather than imposing psychiatric judgment is the more supportive stance. Whatever they represent, those experiences were very important to the dying patients who had them. We need to examine more carefully the impact of context on the dying process. Context includes the quality of advocacy and nonjudgmental caring offered by family and staff. Contextual as well as psychobiological factors may significantly influence the altered state experiences of the dying patient. We may discover that we are dealing not only with the "fact of communication with the dead," whether literal or not, but also with the issue of how we and our patients relate to those experiences. We would do well to re-

member that when Goethe was about to die he cried, "Light, light, the world needs more light." It was many years later that Unamuno responded, "Goethe was wrong; what he should have said was 'Warmth, the world needs more warmth.' We shall not die from the darkness, but from the cold."

3. Robert Kastenbaum (1977) notes that "the happily, happily theme threatens to draw attention away from the actual situations of the dying person, their loved ones and their care givers over the days, weeks, and months preceding death. What happens up to the point of that fabulous transition from life to death recedes into the background. This could not be more unfortunate." Will our aversion to death take yet another form and leave us prey to promises of life after death which we cannot integrate emotionally? It is certainly feasible that we run the risk of once again denying death and perhaps biasing our level of care to those who are dying. Will our "knowledge of life after death" leave us in a position to "abandon life-saving efforts for some people, try less hard to save lives at critical moments" (Kastenbaum, 1977)?

> It is hard to have patience with people who say "There is no death" or "Death doesn't matter." There is death, and whatever happens has consequences, and it and they are irrevocable and irreversible. You might as well say that birth doesn't matter. I look up at the night sky. Is anything more certain than that in all those vast times and spaces, if I were allowed to search them, I should nowhere find her face, her voice, her touch? She died. She is dead. Is the word so difficult to learn? (Lewis, 1961)

C. S. Lewis astutely observes that whether we view death as annihilation or transition, it is a real and often monumental event. An emotional blow associated with a change of form. Those I love in the form I love no longer exist. Those having near-death experiences exuberantly extol the virtues of loving and caring for one's fellow man. So let us have the courage to realize that death often will be a bitter pill to swallow. Our pain will almost always accompany the deaths of those we most love. Our wish will almost always be that help and caring are available.

> Real care is not ambiguous. Real care excludes indifference and is the opposite of apathy. The word "care" finds its roots in the gothic "Kara"

which means "to lament." The basic meaning of care is: to grieve, to experience sorrow, to cry out with. I am very much struck by this background of the word care, because we tend to look at caring as an attitude of the strong toward the weak, of the powerful toward the powerless, of the haves toward the have-nots. And, in fact, we feel quite uncomfortable with an invitation to enter into someone's pain before doing something about it. . . . Still, when we honestly ask ourselves which persons in our lives mean the most to us, we often find that it is those who, instead of giving much advice, solutions, or cures, have chosen rather to share our pain and touch our wounds with a gentle and tender hand. The friend who can be silent with us in a moment of despair or confusion, who can stay with us in an hour of grief and bereavement, who can tolerate not knowing, not curing, not healing and face with us the reality of our powerlessness, that is the friend who cares. . . . Our tendency is to run away from the painful realities or to try to change them as soon as possible. But cure without care makes us into rulers, controllers, manipulators, and prevents a real community from taking shape. Cure without care makes us preoccupied with quick changes, impatient and unwilling to share each other's burden. And so cure can often become offending instead of liberating. It is therefore not so strange that cure is not seldom refused by people in need. . . . Those who can sit in silence with their fellow man not knowing what to say but knowing that they should be there, can bring new life in a dying heart. Those who are not afraid to hold a hand in gratitude, to shed tears in grief, and to let a sign of distress arise straight from the heart, can break through paralyzing boundaries and witness the birth of a new fellowship, the fellowship of the broken. (Nouwen, 1974)

## The Story of Larry

Larry was an ex-marine, twenty years old, who was dying of acute adult leukemia.[4] In the later stages of his illness, Larry frequently asked whether I believed in a life after death, and if so, in what form. We spent hours discussing the purpose of his life (and mine), whether he (Larry) and I (Charlie) would ever meet again, in a recognizable form, in another time and place. We spoke of loving people, of relationships, of the pain inherent in confusing roles (such as patient, psychologist, or doctor) with people. Larry's limited life span gave the interchange an urgency and vitality absent elsewhere. We were two representatives of the somewhat odd and physically vulnerable species Homo sapiens struggling to understand why we were sitting (or lying) on an oblate spheroid whirling somewhere in the Milky Way. It was frightening and exhilarating, and I'll not likely forget those shared struggles. Perhaps the content didn't matter at all. Perhaps we were only defining our relationship while protecting each other from the Void like children huddling together in the dark . . . perhaps . . . perhaps . . . perhaps.

As his disease progressed, Larry grew weaker and his family, sensing the outcome, withdrew emotionally. While I, too, was bracing myself for the worst, I remained with Larry, discussing those things that were uppermost in his mind. He suggested that I take notes so that I might subsequently use his story in teaching health professionals. When I agreed, Larry seemed to know that his painful drama might positively effect the experiences of other seriously ill people.

I saw Larry on Friday before returning home, and we talked about pain, both emotional and physical, loneliness, and the fact that he felt his family withdrawing. He also felt the staff withdrawing and was enormously saddened by the fact that his physician and favorite nurses were now visiting less frequently. He repeatedly thanked me for being "the one person who was not afraid to share this awful pain" and asked if there was any way he could repay me. I assured him that I had been repaid many times over, but Larry insisted on giving me something. I asked him to be my teacher and translate his experiences for me. "When you're alone, Larry, what thoughts and feelings do you have?" "Specifically, what is it that makes you afraid?" "Teach me how to best help you." In a situation that I have since encountered many times, Larry faded in and out of waking consciousness. In lucid moments, he was extremely clear in responding to my questions, but then would drift into a sleeplike state. He taught me much during that period, and I know I was a support to him as well.

Shortly before I left that Friday, I sat watching Larry with his black and blue body, sunken eyes, and yellow skin. As he lay there with his intravenous "life support," I thought of Auschwitz and Treblinka, my grandfather Aaron, and Viet Nam. Suddenly, as if sensing my despair, Larry awoke, looked straight at me, and said, "I have something very important to say to people who read your book." I listened carefully, somewhat surprised by Larry's intensity. Finally he said, "Dying alone is not easy." There was a calm and clear tone to Larry's message that was uncanny, and he smiled peacefully, adding to my uneasiness. His words haunted me for days. The following Monday I hurried to visit him again. When I arrived at the nurses' station, I was told that Larry had died. I was sad, angry, relieved, confused. Finally I was left with the feeling that somehow I should have known that what Larry was really saying on Friday was "goodbye." Yet it didn't feel like goodbye. There was a tranquil and accepting look on Larry's face, so remarkably discontinuous with those tormented, pain-wracked experiences I had witnessed previously. I believe that what Larry was communicating to me that Friday was "Dying alone is not easy, but the job is done, and I've reached a place of peace. . . . I appreciate and love you for what you've shared with me, and if by chance we meet again. . . ."

## Notes

1. This extract is reprinted from D. Goleman, "Back from the Brink," *Psychology Today*, April 1977, pp. 56–59. Copyright © 1977 Ziff-Davis Publishing Company. Used with permission.

2. K. Osis and E. Haraldsson, *At The Hour of Our Death*. New York: Avon, 1977.

3. This following section is from K. Pelletier and C. Garfield, *Consciousness: East and West*. New York: Harper & Row, 1976.

4. This section is a portion of my paper entitled "The Impact of Death on the Healthcare Professional," in H. Feifel, ed., *New Meanings of Death. New York: McGraw-Hill, 1977.*

## References

Garfield, C., "Consciousness Alteration and Fear of Death," *Journal of Transpersonal Psychology*, 1975, 7, 147–175.

Garfield, C., "The Impact of Death on the Healthcare Professional," in H. Feifel, ed., *New Meanings of Death*. New York: McGraw-Hill, 1977 (a).

Garfield, C., *Rediscovery of the Body: A Psychosomatic View of Life and Death*. New York: Dell, 1977 (b).

Garfield, C., *Psychosocial Care of the Dying Patient*. New York: McGraw-Hill, 1978.

Goleman, D., "Back From the Brink," *Psychology Today*, April, 1977, pp. 56–59.

Heywood, R., "Attitudes to Death in the Light of Dreams and Other Out-of-the-Body Experience," in A. Toynbee, ed., *Man's Concern with Death*. New York: McGraw-Hill, 1968.

James, W., *The Varieties of Religious Experience*. New York: New American Library of World Literature, 1958.

Jones, E., *Free Associations*. New York: Hogarth, 1959.

Jung, C., *Memories, Dreams, Reflections*. New York: Random House, 1961.

Kastenbaum, R., "Temptations from the Ever After," *Human Behavior*, 1977, 6, 28–33.

Kastenbaum, R., and Aisenberg, R., *The Psychology of Death*. New York: Springer, 1972.

Koestler, A., "Cosmic Consciousness," *Psychology Today*, April, 1977, pp. 51–54, 104.

Kuhn, T., *The Structure of Scientific Revolutions*. Chicago: University of Chicago Press, 1962.

Lewis, C. S., *A Grief Observed*. New York: Seabury, 1961.

McCain, G., and Segal, E., *The Games of Science*. Belmont, Calif.: Brooks Cole, 1969.

Nouwen, H., *Out of Solitude*. Notre Dame, Ind.: Ave Maria Press, 1974.

Osis, K., *Deathbed Observations of Physicians and Nurses*. New York: Parapsychology Foundation, 1961.

Osis, K., and Haraldsson, E., *At the Hour of Death*. New York: Avon, 1977.

Pelletier, K., and Garfield, C., *Consciousness: East and West*. New York: Harper & Row, 1976.

Polanyi, M., *Tacit Knowing*. London: Routledge & Kegan Paul, 1967.

Tart, C., "Scientific Foundations for the Study of Altered States of Consciousness," *Journal of Transpersonal Psychology*, 1972, 3, 93–124.

# 5

# Contacting the Dead: Does Group Identification Matter?

*Richard A. Kalish*

*There are two common ways of examining orientations toward death. One is to focus on the individual. What are this particular person's thoughts about dying, death, or the dead? The other is to focus on large populations. What do Americans think of dying, death, or the dead? How about old people? Men as compared with women? The mentally ill and the "normal"? Each of these approaches has its place. However, both neglect another level of reality that Richard A. Kalish treats in this chapter.*

*Exclusive attention to the individual fails to consider his or her relationship to society. What we take to be individual dynamics might be more properly understood as the individual's participation in culturally shared dynamics. And yet to treat an entire society or one of its major components as monolithic is to invite another type of oversimplification, the sort we often describe as stereotyping.*

*Kalish reminds us of the importance of sub- (and even subsubsub-) cultures as mediators for the individual's orientation toward dying, death, and the dead. His presentation draws upon some of his own research findings in an area that has yet to be studied extensively. The author proves himself to be a member of that small subsubsubsubculture of ethnically sensitive "social thanatologists," if such a term be admissable.*

Adapted from "Contacting the Dead: Empirical Issues," a paper presented to the 85th Annual Convention of the American Psychological Association, San Francisco, 1977.

The obvious answer to the query in the title is "Of course." The groups to which you belong, whether by accident of birth or by choice, have a great deal to do with your views and experiences involving contacts with people known to be dead.

People frequently ask about "the American view of contacting the dead or communicating with the dead." *The* American view of anything is nonexistent. One cannot understand a complex culture—and perhaps all cultures are complex cultures—through broad generalizations. Within our culture, as within every culture, are innumerable subcultures as well as other groups that help shape attitudes, beliefs, values, and perceptions of experience.

To carry this a step further: Within every subculture are additional subsubcultures and within these are immense individual differences, so that no matter how we refine the unit of society to which we refer, there will be error and variability. It still would seem acceptable to make generalizations about these units, as long as we don't explicitly or implicitly assume that we represent all Cherokee indians, all drivers of heavy equipment, or all displaced homemakers merely because we have data, even good data, on one or three or seven groups having a characteristic.

This chapter will focus on what 434 adult residents of Greater Los Angeles said about their own contacts with people they knew were dead. These 434 persons will be viewed from the perspective of their ethnic/racial community, their age, their sex, their educational level, and their self-evaluated religious devoutness, but with particular emphasis on ethnicity and age.

In our attempts to show that there is no single American view of communicating with the dead, we are most concerned to avoid the suggestion that there is a single black American attitude, a single middle-aged attitude, or a single middle-aged black attitude. For any group or subgroup, there are modal positions, views that deviate from modal positions, and a range of positions. It is important to consider them all.

## The Shelves of Bookstores

The shelves of university bookstores are filled with volumes describing experiences of those who have returned from near death or, in some instances, who have claimed to have viewed death, usually their own death. For both kinds of events, the authors record large numbers of instances in which people report a direct encounter with someone who has already died: the dead parents on the opposite shore trying to encourage the presumably dying person to join them, the deceased spouse who returns for a final conversation preliminary to reunion. The kinds of experiences seem to follow consistent themes, and there can be little doubt about the sincerity of the individuals reporting the events.

All this has served the needs of many who gave up their hopes for an afterlife when they found their religious heritages incompatible with their present philosophies. These recent books link their evidence either to scientific and empirical methods or to a quasi-religiosity that does not demand much from its followers—or often both. It is obvious that many authors have rushed to take advantage of a growing market, and their books show evidence of their haste.

In a very few instances, however, the authors have written with care, attempted to document their points adequately, described their methods and findings, and made interpretations with caution (for example, Moody, 1976; Osis and Haraldsson, 1977). Although I am entitled to take issue with these authors—and indeed do take issue with both their procedures and their interpretations of their findings—I am satisfied that the two volumes have made a significant contribution to knowledge. (It is of more than parenthetical interest to students of social movements to observe how many of these books have introductions written by Elisabeth Kübler-Ross.)

In spite of the many authors who claim to be scientific, only Osis does a job thorough enough to evaluate both procedures and findings (Osis, 1961; Osis and Haraldsson, 1977). In his 1977 book he provides a meaningful analysis of the settings in which the death-related experiences happened, the health conditions under which they occurred, and the age, sex, vocation, and so forth of the research participants. He also carefully describes changes in mood, some personality variables, and other characteristics of those involved. Further, he made a cross-cultural comparison by including the results of a 1973 study he helped conduct in India juxtaposed with two surveys (unfortunately, both completed in the early 1960s) in the United States.

Osis also discusses the more specific circumstances of personal communication with someone who has died, while the other authors expend most of their efforts on establishing the validity of life after death. He seems to assume such communication to be a familiar occurrence, but his methodology did not permit him to evaluate the extent to which it does occur.

## The Study

I had also been sufficiently intrigued by this matter to have included several relevant questions as part of a study of death attitudes that David K. Reynolds and I had conducted in the Greater Los Angeles area (described in more detail in Kalish and Reynolds, 1976). As far as I know, this is the first, perhaps still the only, comprehensive study in which a well-selected sample of individuals from a general population describe their experiences with persons who had already died.

Because of the nature of the broader study, Reynolds and I did a careful analysis of our findings by ethnicity, focusing on black Americans, Japanese-Americans, Mexican-Americans, and an Anglo (white) comparison group. An earlier analysis of these data is available in Kalish and Reynolds (1973).

To summarize the procedures briefly: We surveyed 434 adults, divided approximately equally among three ethnic groups and an Anglo comparison group, among three age groups, and among women and men. Social class differences were minimized by the sampling procedures. All interviews were conducted by persons of the same ethnic/racial background as the respondent and, in the case of Japanese or Spanish, in the language of the respondent if it were appropriate. The sampling methods tended to overrepresent the elderly and those who lived in areas of high ethnic density rather than in primarily ethnically integrated sections of the county.

You can see the results in Table 5-1. Over half of the women and over one-third of the men had either "experienced or felt the presence of [some]one after he had died." The experience most often took place in a dream (this dream was explicitly described as not being a "real dream"), but actual visits from the dead person were not uncommon. When communication occurred, the dead person was either seen or heard, only occasionally was he merely "felt" psycho-

## Table 5-1
### Reported Experiences with the Dead

| Question/Response | Ethnicity | | | | Age | | | Sex | |
|---|---|---|---|---|---|---|---|---|---|
| | B.A. | J.A. | M.A. | A.A.* | 20–39 | 40–59 | 60+ | M | F |
| 126 Have you ever experienced or felt the presence of anyone after he had died?  Yes | 55 | 29 | 54 | 38 | 41 | 45 | 46 | 37 | 51 |
| | | (.001) | | | | (n.s.) | | (.01) | |
| 127 (If "Yes") What type of experience?† | | | | | | | | | |
| Dream | 65 | 63 | 74 | 45 | 55 | 64 | 34 | 68 | 60 |
| Visit | 29 | 6 | 21 | 42 | 29 | 25 | 22 | 17 | 32 |
| Seance | 0 | 0 | 3 | 3 | 2 | 3 | 0 | 1 | 2 |
| Other | 6 | 31 | 2 | 11 | 15 | 9 | 5 | 14 | 7 |
| | | (.001) | | | | (n.s.) | | (.10) | |
| 128 What was the quality of the experience?† | | | | | | | | | |
| Appeared/spoke | 68 | 69 | 75 | 82 | 71 | 67 | 83 | 80 | 68 |
| Psychologically felt | 26 | 25 | 16 | 16 | 23 | 26 | 12 | 15 | 25 |
| Sensed by touch | 6 | 6 | 8 | 3 | 6 | 7 | 5 | 5 | 7 |
| | | (n.s.) | | | | (n.s.) | | (.05) | |
| 129 How did you feel at the time?† | | | | | | | | | |
| Pleasant | 55 | 41 | 57 | 63 | 41 | 59 | 66 | 62 | 50 |
| Fearful | 31 | 19 | 36 | 13 | 41 | 22 | 17 | 19 | 33 |
| Mystical | 7 | 16 | 3 | 13 | 8 | 9 | 9 | 8 | 9 |
| Other | 8 | 25 | 3 | 11 | 11 | 10 | 9 | 11 | 9 |
| | | (.01) | | | | (.10) | | (n.s.) | |

*B.A. = Black American; J.A. = Japanese-American; M.A. = Mexican-American; A.A. = Anglo-American
†Based on those responding "Yes" to #126, N=193.

logically. And the experience was much more likely to be pleasant than frightening, especially for men and older persons. Only rarely did other people who were present share the experience.

Although overall age differences were not found, ethnic differences were substantial. Blacks and Mexican-Americans were much more likely to have had this experience than whites who, in turn, were more likely to have communicated with a dead person than Japanese-American respondents. The type of experience also differed. When whites did experience the phenomenon, it tended to be a visit rather than a dream, and the dead person was more likely to have been seen or heard rather than sensed psychologically (although differences here are fairly small and not significant). Further, blacks and Mexican-Americans reported the experience as frightening much more often than Japanese- and white Americans.

Osis and Haraldsson (1977) provided a much more elaborate interview schedule than we had the opportunity to perform. They asked a variety of questions about the characteristics of the "apparition" as well as about the individual who described the encounter. Not only did they include basic demographic data, but they asked about the health condition of the person interviewed at the time of the encounter.

Because of the way Osis collected his data, it is difficult to offer any meaningful comparisons between his findings and ours. However, both studies showed roughly 60 percent of nonterminally ill persons reporting such experiences were women, which coincides, according to Osis, with other studies making male-female comparisons on this issue. (The major emphasis of Osis's work, however, was with people who were terminally ill, and among such individuals sex differences were minimal.)

A further breakdown of the ethnic/racial data produces some interesting findings, although the small numbers in each chi-square cell require caution in interpretation and generalizing. Thus, I mentioned before that blacks and Mexican-Americans were much more likely to encounter a dead person than Japanese- or white Americans. This is primarily because of the middle-aged and elderly blacks and the elderly whites. That is, among Japanese- and Mexican-Americans there are no age differences. Among black Americans the elderly were much more likely to have encountered the presence of a dead person than the middle-aged, who were, in turn, much more likely to have had this experience than the young (elderly black Americans were more likely than any other age-by-ethnicity group to have encountered a dead person). Among white Americans the elderly were considerably less likely to have had this experience (elderly white Americans were eleventh of the twelve age-by-ethnicity groups in this regard). Although age differences did not reach statistical significance for the white Americans, they were significant at the 5 percent level of confidence for the black Americans.

Neither the type of experience (dream, visit) nor the nature of the experience (physically sensed, psychologically sensed) differed by age within any of the ethnic groups. All chi-square tests of statistical significance were low. In addition, each ethnic group displayed the same age-related trend for finding the experience pleasant: a linear trend indicating that the older the person, the more likely he or she was to perceive the experience favorably. Although none of the chi-squares reached statistical significance, they were all substantially in the expected direction. Further, when only the variables *pleasant* and *fearful* were included, the overall chi-square for age was statistically significant.

Education also proved to be a significant variable. The more education an individual had, the less likely he or she was to have experienced an encounter of the sort described. While over half (54 percent) of those with no high school had contact with a dead person and nearly half (49 percent) of those with some high school had also experienced the encounter, less than half (42 percent) of the high school graduates and fewer than a third (31 percent) of the people having attended college reported the experience. The differences were statistically significant ($p < .01$), and the meaning seems equally significant. We cannot determine how much of the educational differences are attributable to the greater number of Mexican-Americans who were more likely both to have limited education and to report communication with the deceased, but the trends clearly indicate that even without these people education is inversely related to reporting contact with a dead person.

Other educational differences are difficult to interpret. People who attended college were least likely to report having experienced the contact through a dream and most likely to describe their experience as mystical, rather than either pleasant or fearful. The people with the least education most often described what happened as fearful or in otherwise negative terms and most often talked about having had the experience in a dreamlike state. However, numbers in these instances are small, and we wish to report the findings only as suggestive and no more.

Apparently, education either limits the possibility of openness to this experience, limits a person's willingness to discuss the experience, or limits the interpretations of what constitutes the experience.

Our analysis of religiousness as a factor produced relatively little information, somewhat to our surprise. Correlations with items that we felt represented religious beliefs were very low or nonexistent (we must point out, however, that we did not have any direct measures of religious beliefs). We also asked people to compare their own religiousness with that of others of roughly their age, sex, and ethnicity. Of those who felt themselves more religious in this comparison, 35 percent had reported contact with the dead; of those describing themselves as less religious, 42 percent did so; of those who believed themselves about the same as their reference group, 52 percent had contact with a dead person.

We are not certain what this curvilinear relationship represents, but it did produce a statistically significant chi-square ($p < .05$), and we report the data to enable others to integrate it into their own work. Osis and Haraldsson (1977) interpreted their data as indicating that more religious persons were more likely to have this experience, but they admitted that their evidence was sketchy.

One additional data analysis: We intercorrelated seventy-five items to determine what kinds of relationships existed among the items. Since the large number of participants permits a relatively small correlation to become statistically significant, we looked only at correlations above 0.20 for this presentation. Only four items qualified on this basis, but each of the four makes logical sense and also adds some understanding of the phenomenon. (All correlations were between 0.20 and 0.23.)

Persons who had encountered someone who had died were also significantly more likely to have had on at least one occasion "the unexplainable feeling" that they were going to die themselves.

They were also more likely to have had the same feeling about someone else. And they were more likely than average to have felt close to dying themselves. The fourth significant item was their tendency to believe that people dying of cancer sense their condition without being told.

What emerges, then, is that having an encounter with a dead person is modal behavior for certain groups in the population (blacks in general and elderly blacks in particular, Mexican-Americans in general, people with under nine years of formal schooling in general, women in general) and atypical for other groups (middle-aged Japanese-Americans, elderly white Americans, for whom the figures fell below 30 percent). Not only do individuals reporting these experiences differ in demographic characteristics, but they also differ in other ways: They are more likely to have had other kinds of mystical or paranormal feelings and experiences concerning their own deaths and the deaths of others and they have had premonitions about death and believe that others can sense their own deaths as well.

Even allowing for the possible distortions in sampling (for example, oversampling the elderly and those living in areas of high ethnic density, limiting respondents to Greater Los Angeles), it seems apparent that this experience, far from being unusual or pathological even in our general culture, is familiar and may well be considered normative. In some groups within our culture, it is unequivocally familiar and normative.

## Questions and Speculations

A number of unanswered questions inevitably emerge. For example, why did the frequency of reporting an encounter with the dead drop with age among white Americans? Was this just a chance factor, or is there a better explanation? Also, what proportion of encounters occurred shortly after the death of a loved person? Unfortunately, we did not ask that question directly, but we would have predicted that the incidence of such experiences would have increased with age. That it did not, except among blacks, leads us to believe that widows and other people who have lost intimate relationships do not account for as large a proportion of the experiences as we had anticipated.

I would hypothesize, however, that the event we have been discussing did reflect an experience with a dead spouse, sibling, parent, or even child when the person reporting the experience was elderly, but that this was not so often the case among younger and middle-aged research participants. This could also explain why older people in each ethnic group reported the experience as more pleasant and less frightening than younger people. That is, since for the elderly respondent, the deceased person whose presence was perceived was presumably a loved one, the experience was positive. For younger participants, the encounter was with someone with whom the past relationship was threatening and much less intimate, and therefore postdeath contact was also threatening. This, of course, is highly speculative. (Osis and Haraldsson found that younger people were more likely to have encountered people of the previous generation, while older people experienced those of their own generation more often.)

Throughout the larger study from which the present data were drawn, the greatest intergenerational differences were found between older blacks and younger blacks, so it is not surprising that they also differed on sensing the presence of a dead person. This difference probably reflects the increased secularization of the latter, at least in the Los Angeles area. Since both blacks and Mexican-Americans are permitted by their value systems to communicate with the dead, as are—to a lesser extent—Japanese- and white Americans, there is no suggestion at all in the data that any form of pathology is involved.

Some speculations now seem in order. For some people communicating with a dead person is consonant with their value system. The nature of the communication may be frightening, but the fact that such communication occurred is not in itself perceived as threatening or an indication of mental illness. Mental health professionals need to consider how to enable these people to deal with their fears without in any way questioning the validity of their experiences.

Others who have these experiences do not have value systems that lend ready acceptance to what they have perceived. Undoubtedly, psychologists should recognize the frequency with which such events happen and do their best to allay any anxieties that such people may have. Obviously, the event means something, but that something is rarely pathological.

I have avoided up until now discussing my beliefs in these matters. I will now state them briefly. I do not believe that these people have engaged in communication with the dead, and I do not believe that the people described by Moody (1976), by Elisabeth Kübler-Ross in many talks, and by others actually had died. However, I do believe that the experiences are both very vivid and seem very real, that they are neither dreams nor indication of emotional disturbance. Rather, they are signals that the intensity of the loss or other experience is extremely great and extremely enduring, and that the previously formed associations with the dead person were extremely strong. As a result, minimal stimuli in the form of a familiar room or chair or even in the form of a memory become sufficient to recreate an apparent reality in the form of the person who has died.

## A Few Final Thoughts

It is obvious that at least some individuals in each of the groups we interviewed believed they had experienced a meeting with one or more persons who had died. This occurred regardless of age, sex, ethnicity, education, or self-evaluated religiousness, although not to the same extent for each group. What the data do not tell us is what the experience meant to the experiencing individual. A young black man devoutly attached to the African Methodist Episcopal church and a college graduate may experience the visit of his recently deceased mother; an elderly Japanese-American woman, casually identifying as a Buddhist and with nine years of public school in Japan, also experiences the visit of her mother who died some twenty years earlier. Age, ethnicity, sex, education, and the religious belief system may all enter into the way in which the meeting is experienced and the influence it has on the participant after the experience is over.

Further, it is a gross mistake to assume that only blacks, Hispanics, and persons of Asian ancestry can have these experiences. There are major and obvious divisions within these groups: The black from Jamaica is much different from the black born and reared in Chicago; the man who escaped from Castro's Cuba does not share all the values of a migratory worker from nothern Mexico; the Catholic or Moslem Filipine-American man or woman differs greatly from the Buddhist/Shinto or Christian Japanese-American man or woman.

And, of course, ethnicity is a factor for people who trace their ancestry to Germany, Italy, Greece, or Russia, for those who consider themselves Jews, Armenians, or Slavs. Each of these individuals has been socialized, whether in 1910 or 1960, to the meaning of communicating with a dying person; each has heard myths and folk legends, has read fairy tales and novels, that bear on the issue. Each is caught, albeit in differing ways, between the present-day emphasis on rationalism, empiricism, and scientism and the traditional views of religion and faith. As each ethnic community blends into the general American model, its members still retain some flavor from their origins, and the significance of ghosts, apparitions, "presences," and other forms of communicating with the dead are very much part of these origins.

## References

Kalish, R. A., and Reynolds, D. K., "Phenomenological Reality and Post-death Contact," *Journal for the Scientific Study of Religion*, 1973, 12, 209–221.

Kalish, R. A., and Reynolds, D. K., *Death and Ethnicity: A Psychocultural Study*. Los Angeles: University of Southern California Press, 1976.

Moody, R. A., *Life After Life*. New York: Bantam, 1976.

Osis, K., *Deathbed Observations by Physicians and Nurses*. New York: Parapsychology Foundation, 1961.

Osis, K., and Haraldsson, E., *At the Hour of Death*. New York: Avon, 1977.

# 6

# Near-Death Experiences: Their Interpretation and Significance

*Russell Noyes, Jr.*

*Alive one moment—but perhaps dead the next. How does a person think and feel in the midst of a life-threatening situation? Psychiatrist Russell Noyes, Jr., has studied responses to near-death experiences in a variety of circumstances, including falls, drownings, and accidents, as well as illness. Interesting though the information is on a descriptive level, Noyes presses on to a possible explanation.*

*Depersonalization is a central concept here. Noyes suggests that "the depersonalized state is one that mimics death." The threatened individual psychologically escapes death "for what has already happened cannot happen again; he cannot die because he is already dead." Other key concepts for Noyes are the state of* hyperalertness *and the generation of* panoramic memory *in the life-or-death crisis situation.*

*Here is a careful and sensitive analysis of the human response to immediate mortal danger, one that respects experiential data but attempts to draw its principles from dynamics already known in the broad realm of human behavior rather than invoke mysterious concepts to explain mysterious events. However Noyes's theory may hold up against the test of time, it offers a lucid and provocative approach for us today.*

In 1892 a Swiss geology professor, Albert Heim, published a report describing the subjective experiences of people who had survived falls in the Alps.[11] Based on over thirty accounts he claimed that in nearly every instance a similar mental state developed, which he characterized dramatically as follows:

> There was no anxiety, no trace of despair, no pain; but rather calm seriousness, profound acceptance, and a dominant mental quickness and sense of surety. Mental activity became enormous, rising to a hundred-fold velocity or intensity. The relationships of events and their probable outcomes were overviewed with objective clarity. No confusion entered at all. Time became greatly expanded. . . . In many cases there followed a sudden review of the individual's entire past; and finally the person falling often heard beautiful music and fell in a superbly blue heaven containing roseate cloudlets.[11]

Heim avoided speculative interpretation of these accounts, offering them instead, by way of consolation, to the families of mountain-climbing accident victims. Almost forty years later Pfister published a psychoanalytic study of near-death experiences based largely on Heim's material.[28] He believed that they represented profound regression and denial of death, a view later shared by Hunter.[12] However, with these exceptions, Heim's initial study received little notice.[17]

Recently the author, in collaboration with others, gathered data from over 200 persons regarding their subjective experiences during moments of life-threatening danger.[19-21] Descriptively, they confirmed Heim's original observations. Detailed analysis of accounts and questionnaire data revealed several dimensions to these experiences that appeared meaningful in terms of the endangered personality's response to the threat of death.[24] The purpose of this chapter is to summarize these findings and explore their interpretation. Discussion is focused upon their overall significance and directions for further study.

## Findings

In two reports 215 accounts from 205 people who had encountered life-threatening danger were analyzed.[19, 21, 24] These accounts were obtained through a variety of informal contacts, and seventy-six persons were personally interviewed. In addition 186 completed a forty-item questionnaire that dealt with a variety of subjective phenomena commonly reported during altered states of consciousness. The life-threatening circumstances responsible for reported experiences were as follows: falls, 58; drownings, 54; automobile accidents, 53; miscellaneous accidents, 24; and serious illnesses, 26.

A variety of transient subjective effects were reported by people during their exposure to life-threatening danger. These included changes in the experience of time, space, emotion, sensation, volition, sense of reality, sense of attachment, and memory.[21] These have been described in detail elsewhere but may be summarized as follows: Most people reported that time slowed down and events seemed to occur in slow motion.[19, 21] Many described a calm, emotionless state despite accurate perception of danger. A number even felt like detached observers of themselves and the events taking place around them. A feeling of strangeness or unreality was often recalled, and some claimed that the world around them seemed strangely foreign. Diminished vision, hearing, and bodily sensation were also described. Many people reported that their movements and thoughts seemed to occur automatically without effort on their part.

In contrast to these effects reflecting a dampening of experience, many also reported contrasting effects suggestive of heightened arousal.[23] They described thoughts that were unusually rapid and vivid. Some reported a sense of unusual familiarity (déjà vu). Many claimed heightened perception together with increased acuity of vision and hearing. The attention of persons so alerted was focused on the dangerous environment as they made efforts to rescue themselves. When circumstances became overwhelming or rescue efforts were given up, attention was often redirected toward inner experience, including revival of memories (panoramic memory) and effects typical of mystical consciousness.[19, 24] The latter consisted of a sense of harmony or unity, a feeling of great understanding, intense positive emotion, and a feeling of being controlled by an outside force.

Table 6-1 shows the frequency with which various subjective effects were reported on the questionnaire designed for that purpose.[24] People in the midst of an accident, who believed themselves about to die, reported a number of mystical items and revival of

Table 6-1
Subjective Effects Resulting from Near-Death Experiences

| | Percentage of Subjects | |
| --- | --- | --- |
| | Believed About to Die | Believed Not About to Die |
| | $N=117$ | $N=68$ |
| 1. Altered passage of time | 78 | 65 |
| 2. Self strange or unreal | 74 | 57* |
| 3. Thoughts speeded | 69 | 58 |
| 4. Thoughts sharp or vivid | 68 | 51* |
| 5. Thoughts, movements mechanical | 61 | 54 |
| 6. Detachment from world | 61 | 44* |
| 7. Loss of emotion | 51 | 54 |
| 8. Vision, hearing sharper | 40 | 35 |
| 9. Detachment from body | 40 | 32 |
| 10. Objects small, far away | 35 | 27 |
| 11. Revival of memories | 45 | 13* |
| 12. Strange bodily sensations | 39 | 24* |
| 13. Controlled by outside force | 32 | 25 |
| 14. Body apart from self | 33 | 22 |
| 15. World strange or unreal | 28 | 30 |
| 16. Wall between self and emotions | 26 | 27 |
| 17. Feeling of great understanding | 33 | 18* |
| 18. Sense of harmony or unity | 28 | 24 |
| 19. Colors or visions | 32 | 15* |
| 20. Images sharp or vivid | 28 | 8* |
| 21. Strange sounds | 20 | 12 |
| 22. Vision, hearing blurred or dull | 12 | 18 |
| 23. Feeling of joy | 19 | 6* |
| 24. Revelation | 14 | 5 |
| 25. Body changed in shape or size | 10 | 12 |
| 26. Thoughts blurred or dull | 12 | 6 |

*indicates significant difference ($p < .05$)

memories more frequently. Age at the time of the experience and loss of consciousness were variables that also influenced the reporting of certain effects. Most of the effects occurred with comparable frequency among a group of hospitalized accident victims who were interviewed without previous knowledge that their subjective experiences were part of another study.[23]

Table 6-2
Dimensions of the Near-Death Experience

FACTOR I*: MYSTICAL

1. Feeling of great understanding                                    .74
2. Images sharp or vivid                                            .72
3. Revival of memories                                              .69
4. Sense of harmony, unity                                          .68
5. Feeling of joy                                                   .68
6. Revelation                                                       .62
7. Controlled by outside force                                      .56
8. Colors or visions                                               .53
9. Strange bodily sensations                                        .44

FACTOR II: DEPERSONALIZATION

1. Loss of emotion                                                  .69
2. Body apart from self                                             .62
3. Self strange or unreal                                           .62
4. Objects small, far away                                          .62
5. Detachment from body                                             .61
6. World strange or unreal                                          .61
7. Wall between self and emotions                                   .61
8. Detachment from world                                            .52
9. Body changed in shape or size                                    .43
10. Strange sounds                                                  .41
11. Altered passage of time                                         .35

FACTOR III: HYPERALERTNESS

1. Thoughts sharp or vivid                                          .69
2. Thoughts speeded                                                 .65
3. Vision, hearing sharper                                          .62
4. Thoughts blurred or dull                                        −.56
5. Altered passage of time                                          .48
6. Thoughts, movements mechanical                                   .41

*Factors include questionnaire items with rotated factor loadings of .35 or greater.

A four-factor analysis of these subjective effects produced three meaningful factors that explained 41 percent of the variance (Table 6-2).[24] Factor I was a mystical factor containing all the mystical items from the questionnaire (feeling of great understanding, sense of harmony or unity, feeling of joy, and revelation). Also included were effects reflecting enhanced visual imagery (images sharp or vivid, colors or visions) that seemed to provide a substrate for panoramic memory (revival of memories). Factor II was a depersonalization factor containing the symptom of depersonalization (a strange or unreal self) and other effects previously identified as belonging to this syndrome (objects small, far away; detachment from body; wall between self and emotions; and altered passage of time). Factor III, despite the small number of items, was recognizable as a hyperalertness factor.

Thus, three dimensions of the altered consciousness developing in response to life-threatening danger were distinguished. Very similar factors were identified in a separate study of accident victims, lending support to their existence as meaningful dimensions of this experience.[23] In terms of frequency, hyperalertness effects were reported most frequently (mean frequency 59 percent), followed by depersonalization (mean 39 percent), and mystical effects (mean 26 percent). Hyperalertness and depersonalization appeared to be opposites of one another, a fact made especially clear in the study of accident victims referred to above.[23]

## Interpretation

Because human experience may be conceptualized on different levels, it seems appropriate to approach an interpretation of near-death experiences from more than one level in order to avoid reductionism. From a *physiologic* standpoint one may interpret depersonalization and its contrasting tendency (hyperalertness) in terms of a neural mechanism developing in reaction to dangerous circumstances. According to Roth and Harper, such contrasting effects are manifestations of heightened arousal on the one hand and a dissociation of consciousness from that arousal on the other.[29] Depersonalization may, as they suggest, represent an adaptive mechanism that combines opposing reaction tendencies, the one serving to intensify alertness and the other to dampen potentially disorganizing emotion. This viewpoint was supported by people interviewed who described themselves as functioning effectively under extraordinary circumstances, aided by a sense of calm objectivity.[21] Their claim of little traumatic aftermath may be further evidence of the adaptive nature of this mechanism.

An intimate association between depersonalization and anxiety has been demonstrated.[23] Of course, fear is a natural response to extreme danger and may trigger the instantaneous development of depersonalization. Still, the precise mediator is unknown. Depersonalization may develop in response to anxiety or to the symbolic appreciation of danger. Extreme anxiety is often accompanied cognitively by fear of imminent death; on the other hand, the threat of death may lead to extreme anxiety. The two are intimately associated and, in this sense, both may participate in the development of depersonalization.[21]

On a *psychological* level depersonalization may be interpreted as a defense against the threat of death. Not only did people in the studies described find themselves calm in otherwise frightening situations but they also felt detached from what was happening. This detachment was often described in physical as well as emotional terms, and many people felt like observers rather than participants in the events taking place. Arlow, commenting on the split of the self into participant and observer, hypothesized that the observing self, by dissociating itself from the remainder of the ego, produced a feeling of estrangement, thereby creating the fantasy that danger, though real, was threatening a stranger.[1]

The depersonalized state is one that mimics death. In it a person experiences himself as empty, lifeless, and unfamiliar. In a sense he creates psychologically the very situation that environmental circumstances threaten to impose. In so doing he escapes death, for what has already happened cannot happen again; he cannot die, because he is already dead. An extension of this defense was observed by Dlin among survivors of cardiac arrests who for a time believed themselves dead.[7] They survived, however, as observers of themselves and in this regard shared a tendency to which Freud drew our attention. He noted that death (as annihilation) is unimaginable, and that whenever we attempt to imagine it we perceive of ourselves as spectators.[8]

Thus, the elusive "I," or observer of the self, remains one step away from destruction. As the ego develops, this observing self

separates itself from threatening and uncontrollable forces and remains ready to sacrifice portions of itself in order to survive. Ultimately, in the face of death, it seems prepared to sacrifice the entire
self in a futile attempt to master the unmasterable. Thus, like many
defenses that when used to excess defeat their purpose, the detachment that reaches its height in depersonalization may create a psychological death.

However, in hyperalertness we see an opposite tendency, one
that includes déjà vu, the opposite of the symptom of depersonalization. Were it not for the awkwardness of such terminology, its
effects might be referred to as "personalizing" for, in contrast to
depersonalization, they are accompanied by feelings of intense
arousal and vitality.[23] When rescue efforts are in progress, attention
may be focused on the threatening environment. But when such
efforts are given up, attention may turn inward towards intensified
mental imagery.

During this kind of intense arousal, the focus of attention becomes narrow, and awareness of the broader context of events,
including their location in time, may be lost. The observer is, as it
were, set aside, and experience takes on an unmodified, immediate
quality. In this way it resembles the quality of existence in early life
before ego differentiation. In such a context it is not surprising to
find experiences of a relatively timeless quality being recalled, especially blissful ones. Such moments come largely from early childhood when life was experienced with greatest intensity and time
had only begun to impose its limitations. In a moving passage
describing the death of James Wait, Conrad gives us a glimpse of
this kind of life-affirming immersion of consciousness in the past.

> Wait came back with a start . . . and returned at once to the regions of
> memory that know nothing of time. He felt untired, calm and safely
> withdrawn within himself beyond the reach of every grave incerti-
> tude. . . . He was very quiet and easy amongst his vivid reminiscences
> which he mistook joyfully for images of an undoubted future.[5]

This revival of memories (panoramic memory) appears meaningful in terms of the personality's response to approaching death.[22] The
phenomenon is largely confined to people who during an accident
believe that death is imminent. Sadness is experienced by many and

appears to be a fragmentary expression of grief. The vivid mental images resemble another feature, which according to Parkes, is a pathognomonic feature of that syndrome.[27] Soon after bereavement intense memories of the deceased are reported that represent the bereaved person's clinging to a lost loved one. In life-threatening circumstances a person confronts the loss of himself and becomes absorbed with images of his own past life. Just as bereaved persons cling to symbolic representations of departed loved ones, so dying individuals may develop attachment to memories, symbols of their existence.

Panoramic memory also resembles the reminiscent life review of elderly people.[22] It may, in fact, represent a fleeting and intensified form of the latter. The term "review" refers not only to relooking but to reexamination, an aspect Butler stressed in his interpretation of reminiscence among the aged.[2] He felt that the review brought about a reassessment and integration of life as it neared its end. Consequently, he looked upon it as a positive and health-promoting activity stimulated by disengagement from current life and by the aged person's increasing difficulty in projecting himself into the future. Butler felt the approaching completion of an elderly person's life stimulated the kind of reassessment that commonly occurs in psychotherapy as a new self-image develops. Under the most favorable circumstances this author sees the review process as leading to "acceptance of mortal life, a sense of serenity, and pride in accomplishment."[3] Glimpses of this sort of overall assessment accompany depersonalization in response to life-threatening danger.

While the mystical dimension of near-death experience may be viewed as a still further inward turning of the personality or more complete withdrawal from extreme circumstances, it cannot adequately be interpreted in psychological terms.[15] According to *Webster's Third New International Dictionary*, "mystical" is that which has "spiritual meaning, existence or reality"; hence, it is appropriately interpreted on the *spiritual* level. James identified the hallmarks of mystical consciousness as ineffability, transiency, passivity, and a noetic quality.[13] By passivity he referred to a relinquishing of voluntary control, as if a person's "will were in abeyance, and indeed sometimes as if he were grasped and held by a superior power."[13] By its noetic quality he meant a sense of truth accompanying the experience. "They are," he said, "states of insight into depths of truth unplumbed by the discussive intellect. They are illuminations, revelations, full of significance and importance."[13] Others have added transcendence of time, space, and individual identity, a sense of sacredness, and a deeply felt positive mood. Such deviations of consciousness develop under a wide variety of influences, including sensory deprivation, drug intoxication, and emotional excitation and are subject to varied interpretations, depending upon personal beliefs and the setting in which the experience takes place.[18]

Mystical consciousness appears to represent a separate dimension of near-death experiences, perhaps amounting to a further extension of depersonalization.[17] It appears to develop less frequently than depersonalization and may be a relatively rare occurrence among people exposed to, or dying as a result of, life-threatening danger. Its effects are more commonly reported by people who believe that death is imminent and therefore is associated with a more serious threat to life. In all probability mystical consciousness is more prone to occur among people dying from physical disease, many of whom are experiencing physiologic alterations in consciousness and receiving minimal environmental stimulation, a fertile setting for such experiences.[14, 25, 26]

In one series 23 percent of people reporting near-death encounters attached some religious significance to their brief experiences.[20] For most this was rather fragmentary or tentative. A number, for example, interpreted the sense of detachment to mean that their spirit had left their body. They quite naturally felt they had gained firsthand evidence of the spirit's continuation after death. A few felt that they had momentarily experienced a timeless state or eternity. And a few more identified as the Holy Spirit the force that seemed to influence them. In a limited way six of more than one hundred individuals experienced what might in the loosest sense be called "heaven" and two similarly experienced "hell."

It should not surprise us to find people who have survived encounters with death occasionally reporting mystical experiences of a limited kind. Realization of approaching death (for example, from people who think they are drowning) brings with it an intense emotional response and, in many instances, altered brain physiology. Neither should it surprise us to learn that such experiences are influenced by individual beliefs regarding the transition from this life to the next. The content of altered states of consciousness are modified, regardless of their form, by the experience and expectations of an individual. Thus, the fleeting images of future events reported by accident victims include scenes of their completed accident, of relatives receiving the news of their death, and even of subsequent events such as their own funeral.[22] These are simply vivid representations of anticipated events. Is the content of mystical consciousness occurring just before death similarly determined? We will return to that question.

## Discussion

It can be difficult to gain or maintain proper perspective on a subject such as this one that has become an object of widespread fascination and emotional investment. Meager findings are often given sensational treatment in the news media, and frequently investigators, in response to strong personal biases, forsake rigorous methods and popularize studies in support of their beliefs. At the same time more careful researchers avoid the field, so as not to jeopardize their professional reputations. The subject of near-death experiences is enjoying unprecedented popularity despite minimal data. If we are to perserve it as an area of legitimate research, we must approach it with the same skepticism and methodologic precision that we apply to other areas of scientific inquiry.

The depersonalization syndrome, reported so frequently by people exposed to life-threatening danger, is a familiar psychopathologic entity.[23] It occurs under a wide variety of circumstances, including drug intoxication and sensory deprivation. Certain affective states such as depression and anxiety are also commonly accompanied by depersonalization. Consequently, as far as its interpretation is concerned, it is important to recognize that a very similar, if not identical, syndrome occurs in a wide variety of settings. It is by no means unique to the near-death situation. What seems important to an understanding of depersonalization, however, is our identification of the circumstances in which it most predictably makes its appearance.[23] It approaches fear as a common response to extreme danger. Viewed in its natural setting we cannot help but see its adaptive significance. What we see in psychiatric patients with depersonalization is a mechanism that has gone awry and outlived its usefulness.

An intimate association exists between depersonalization and extreme anxiety or excitation. Although both tend to be transient and subside with the passage of danger, they may persist under certain conditions. Then both are part of the clinical picture of traumatic neurosis.[6] In fact, the psychic numbing described by survivors of disasters appears to be a variant of depersonalization. Here we are dealing with the psychopathology associated with psychic trauma. There is much to be learned in this area about the victim and environmental variables that explain the symptomatic variance in response to traumatic events.

Clearly a confrontation with death, however brief, may have a traumatic aftermath. What is surprising is that the opposite effect, namely, a reduced fear of death, is so often reported.[20, 24] It seems clear that the enormous impact of such experiences may influence behavior in either direction. Such changes are of interest to behavioral scientists and, despite retrospective design, lend themselves to study. For example, are observed changes in behavior related to the subjective experience accompanying an encounter with death, as has been suggested by Garfield, or are they simply due to the encounter itself (that is, the person may have been unconscious)?[9] The fear of death is a rather nebulous concept that should perhaps be avoided in examining the impact of near-death experiences. Attention should be directed instead toward anxiety symptoms and anxious personality traits that are manifest in daily living. Just how the fear of death—the ultimate source of anxiety—influences personality is a subject for empirical investigation. Personality changes resulting from near-death encounters may provide clues to further understanding of this question.[24]

As counselors of the dying, we wish to know about the last moments of life. Are they peaceful, as suggested by early writers who cited examples of near-death experiences as proof that death is not the dreadful encounter we tend to suppose?[16] First of all, we have seen that depersonalization can instantaneously occur in moments of sudden danger and in such situations softens the impact of death. It must be comforting to many to realize that just as denial may hold off the painful awareness of approaching death in cancer patients, so depersonalization may serve a similar function in moments of crisis. However, the truth of the matter is that we know very little about the physical and emotional distress experienced by dying people and what factors are most responsible for its observed variation. Carefully designed surveys of large populations of cancer patients using structured interviews and standard symptom inventories are needed.

But what of the euphoric response reported by a few people during near-death experiences and the "reluctant return" voiced by others.[14, 17, 25] We speak hesitantly about this matter, lest death be made to seem alluring. Most of us regard death as, among other things, a final rest from the trials of life. As such it may be accompanied by a certain sense of relief. A considerable burden may be lifted from some of us, in terms not only of everyday struggles but of uncertainty regarding the future. Such a sense of relief was expressed by a mountaineer who, toward the end of a particularly arduous climb, lost his footing and fell to what he presumed to be his death. He related his almost euphoric sense of relief to a realization that the struggle was over, not only for the day but for a lifetime that for him had been characterized by intense striving.

We may sympathize with this reaction and in that sense look forward to death. What we so often fail to appreciate when we judge the reactions of people on the threshold of death are the overwhelming circumstances—whether the result of illness or accident—that weaken their resolve to continue living and bring them to acceptance of death. Some people who have survived encounters with life's end have even wondered, in looking back, if they lost their will to live, forgetting their distress and sense of helplessness in the face of destructive forces. Thomas Hardy in his poem "A Wasted Illness" captures this sense of half-regret that the distress of dying, which made death welcome, might have to be experienced again.[4] For those of us in good health and living vigorously death has little attraction. But the circumstances near the end of life may make it at least acceptable.

It seems important to note that there are a great variety of near-death experiences. Those studied by the author were reported by

people who were psychologically—but not necessarily physically—
close to death.[24] A different kind of experience has been described
by people who narrowly escaped death from physical illness, cardiac arrest, and so forth.[14, 25, 26] Still other experiences have resulted
from the psychological death produced by hallucinogenic drugs.[10]
Certain interesting similarities can be identified, but striking differences are present as well. Descriptive studies to date have tended to
deal with exceptional experiences. They do not help us to judge the
frequency with which certain phenomena occur nor do they allow
us to gauge the variety of subjective experiences occurring at this
time. Descriptive studies based on unselected populations systematically interviewed are needed in order for us to see the subject in
its full perspective.

How are we to interpret mystical experiences that occasionally
occur as people near death? Do they provide us with evidence of
survival?[16] Certainly we find among them support for widespread
religious and cultural beliefs. Within our society faith in God together with the assurance of a continuing relationship with Him
after death are common, especially in the Christian community. Related notions regarding death that are typical in childhood and linger
into adult life also find confirmation in these experiences. They are
that death is a journey and that we continue to exist although out of
sight and beyond communication. Many people overwhelmingly
confirm these beliefs following near-death experiences. They know
that there is a next world *because they have been there.*

But those of us who only hear of them have difficulty accepting
these experiences as revelations of truth or evidence of survival.
This is because we cannot subject them to the usual methods of
empirical confirmation by which we arrive at public knowledge.
We have progressed little beyond James who, at the turn of the
century, had this to say about what might be revealed during a
mystical experience: "What comes must be sifted and tested, and
run the gauntlet of confrontation with the total content of experience just like what comes from the outer world of sense. Its value
must be ascertained by empirical methods, so long as we are not
mystics ourselves."[13] Still, for the person whose life terminates in a
state of mystical consciousness, the experience may bring fulfillment of cherished beliefs. And just as this person's dying may be a

highly individual act, so his interpretation of a final mystical experience may go unchallenged.

Thus, while we have opened up a fascinating area for further investigation, we have only begun to gather reliable data. We must guard against sensationalism and unwarranted claims while careful study proceeds. A number of the phenomena associated with near-death experiences may best be studied in other settings. Both depersonalization and mystical consciousness occur spontaneously and under circumstances that do not impair a person's ability to report his experiences afterward. Even so, the near-death situation to which Heim drew our attention is unique and appears to have much to teach us about the human response to death.

# References

1. Arlow, J. A., "Depersonalization and Derealization," in *Psychoanalysis: A General Psychology*, R. M. Lowenstein, L. M. Newman, M. Schur, and A. J. Solnit, eds. New York: International Universities Press, 1966.

2. Butler, R. N., "The Life Review: An Interpretation of Reminiscence in the Aged," *Psychiatry*, 1963, *26*, 65–76.

3. Butler, R. N., and Lewis, M. I., *Aging and Mental Health, Positive Psychological Approaches*. St. Louis: C. V. Mosby, 1973, pp. 43–44.

4. *Collected Poems of Thomas Hardy*, New York: Macmillan, 1926, p. 139.

5. Conrad, J., *The Nigger of the Narcissus*, in *The Portable Conrad*. New York: Viking, 1969, p. 431.

6. DSM-III Classification, Draft of March 10, 1977, American Psychiatric Association, Washington, D.C.

7. Dlin, B. M., Stern, A., and Poliakoff, S. J., "Survivors of Cardiac Arrest," *Psychosomatic Medicine*, 1974, *14*, 61–67.

8. Freud, S., *Collected Papers*, vol. 4, *Thoughts for the Times on War and Death*. New York: Basic Books, 1959.

9. Garfield, C. A., "Consciousness Alteration and Fear of Death," *Journal of Transpersonal Psychology*, 1975, *7*, 147–175.

10. Grof, S., and Halifax, J., *The Human Encounter with Death*. New York: Dutton, 1977.

11. Heim, A., "Remarks on Fatal Falls," *Yearbook of the Swiss Alpine Club*, 1892, R. Noyes, Jr., and R. Kletti trans., *Omega*, 1972, *3*, 45–52.

12. Hunter, R. C. A., "On the Experience of Nearly Dying," *American Journal of Psychiatry*, 1967, *124*, 84–88.

13. James, W., *The Varieties of Religious Experience*. London: Longmans, Green, 1929.

14. Moody, R. A., Jr., *Life After Life*. Covington, Ga.: Mockingbird Books, 1975.

15. *Mysticism: Quest or Insanity*, Group for the Advancement of Psychiatry, vol. 12, no. 3, 1977.

16. Noyes, R., Jr., "Dying and Mystical Consciousness," *Journal of Thanatology*, 1971, *1*, 25–41.

17. Noyes, R., Jr., "The Experience of Dying," *Psychiatry*, 1972, *35*, 174–184.

18. Noyes, R., Jr., "Is There New Evidence for Survival After Death?" *The Humanist*, 1977, *31*, 51–53.

19. Noyes, R., Jr., and Kletti, R., "Depersonalization in the Face of Life-threatening Danger: A Description," *Psychiatry*, 1976(a) *39*, 19–27.

20. Noyes, R., Jr., and Kletti, R., "Depersonalization in the Face of Life-threatening Danger: An Interpretation," *Omega*, 1976(b), *7*, 103–114.

21. Noyes, R., Jr., and Kletti, R., "Depersonalization in Response to Life-threatening danger," *Comprehensive Psychiatry*, 1977(a), *18*, 375–384.

22. Noyes, R., Jr., and Kletti, R., "Panoramic Memory: A Response to the Threat of Death," *Omega*, 1977(b), *8*, 181–194.

23. Noyes, R., Jr., Hoenk, P. R., Kuperman, S., and Slymen, D. J., "Depersonalization in Accident Victims and Psychiatric Patients," *Journal of Nervous and Mental Disorders*, 1977, *164*, 401–407.

24. Noyes, R., Jr., and Slymen, D. J., "The Subjective Response to Life-threatening Danger," *Omega*. In press.

25. Osis, K., *Deathbed Observations by Physicians and Nurses*. New York: Parapsychology Foundation, 1961.

26. Osis, K., and Haraldsson, E., *At the Hour of Death*. New York: Avon 1977.

27. Parkes, C. M., *Bereavement, Studies of Grief in Adult Life*. New York: International Universities Press, 1972.

28. Pfister, O., "Shockdenken und shock-phantasien bei höchster todesgefahr," *Internationale zeitschrift für psychoanalyse*, 1930, *16*, 430–455.

29. Roth, M., and Harper, M., "Temporal Lobe Epilepsy and the Phobic Anxiety-Depersonalization Syndrome. Part II: Practical and Theoretical Considerations," *Comprehensive Psychiatry*, 1962, *3*, 215–226.

# Deliberately Induced, Premortem, Out-of-Body Experiences: An Experimental and Theoretical Approach

*Sandor B. Brent*

*So-called out-of-body experiences (OBEs) are among the most dramatic features of the close encounters with death that have been reported to and by Moody, Osis, and others. There are beliefs and theories about the significance of OBEs, but little that can be called firm knowledge. It is known, however, that OBEs are not limited to the near-death situation. They have been associated, for example, with mystic experiences in which no death threat is obvious. But OBEs can also occur in rather ordinary, noncrisis, nonmystical contexts as well. An exploration of the OBE without the physiological crisis and emotional charge of the near-death situation might prove illuminating.*

*Sandor B. Brent is a developmental psychologist who has induced OBEs as a learning exercise in college students well before the phenomenon came to general attention as part of the near-death encounter. His account of the technique and its typical results will interest many readers for its value as an educational maneuver. Additionally, however, his disciplined speculations will stimulate further ideas on basic perceptual phenomena in general and the special phenomena that are the concern of this book. His ideas have the further advantage of lending themselves to well-focused and controlled research.*

> This unstable world of the mind. A world of evanescent impressions; a
> world without matter or spirit, neither objective nor subjective; a world
> without the ideal architecture of space; a world made of time . . . a
> tireless labyrinth, a chaos, a dream.
>
> from *Labyrinths* by Jorges Luis Borges

The term "death" refers to the cessation of the physiological functions of the body, according to *Webster's Third New International
Dictionary*. The question of whether there is "life" after death is,
therefore, a question of whether (1) these physiological functions
can be restored once they have ceased (hence whether corporeal
"resurrection" is possible) or (2) consciousness as we know it can
continue to exist and to function beyond the point at which these
physiological processes have ceased to function.

The physicalistic bias of modern rational thought has led us to
presume that consciousness is a mere derivative, an epiphenome-
non, of the physiological processes themselves, so that when these
physiological processes cease to function, the functions of consciousness itself are presumed to cease as well. On the other hand,
a great many of the traditional literatures of the world (for example,
Budge, 1895/1967; Evans-Wentz, 1957; Kapleau, 1967) as well as the
Christian gospels suggest that consciousness continues to function
for various periods of time after death. Recent reports of life-after-
death experiences (LADEs) occurring in modern urban medical settings (Moody, 1975) have once again raised this age-old issue of
whether the contents and processes of consciousness are logically
merely derivative from, coequal with, or prior to the psychological
processes of the body (cf. Brent, 1978).

This chapter is not concerned with the phenomenon of LADEs in
particular, but with the closely related phenomenon of out-of-body
experiences (OBEs). The investigation of OBEs is closely related to
that of LADEs both because (1) LADEs are typically accompanied
by OBEs and (2) both experiences typically involved a distinct
*awareness of the absence* of any bodily experiences whatsoever.

I wish to express my appreciation to Dr. Robert Kastenbaum for his encouragement
in the pursuit of this work, and to the University of Michigan-Wayne State University Institute of Gerontology for the support that they have provided during various
phases of the preparation of this chapter. Dr. Karl Pribram and Ms. Kathryn Domu-
rath made some valuable suggestions. I am, of course, solely responsible for the
content.

The modern study of OBEs has to date depended primarily on anecdotal reports of events that arise in a relatively spontaneous and unpredictable way as a result of unknown factors operating in an uncontrolled fashion (Monroe, 1973). This has made an experimental approach to the study of OBEs difficult. "Disembodiment" experiences somewhat similar to OBEs have sometimes been deliberately induced through the use of various consciousness-expanding chemicals or as the result of other complex laboratory procedures (for example, extended periods of "sensory deprivation"). However, these procedures themselves and the side effects that they often produce are generally so complex that systematic investigations involving large numbers of individuals are impractical.

The main purpose of this chapter is to report a technique that reliably induces a set of phenomenological experiences formally analogous to OBEs. The heart of this technique is a standardized set of easily administered verbal instructions. Since no special equipment is needed, and since there are no obvious side effects and often very pleasant aftereffects (see below), no special "settings" are required. This technique may therefore provide the basis for a new and more convenient approach to the experimental investigation of certain aspects of OBEs.

## Background

I have used the procedure that I will describe over the past ten years with perhaps as many as twenty different groups of clients and of students. These groups have ranged in size from about four or five up to fifty and more individuals.

This technique was originally designed to aid participants in sensitivity-training and encounter groups in achieving a concrete sense that they are not merely the passive recipients of their conscious experiences but are rather active agents in the construction of these experiences. I have subsequently employed this technique as a teaching device in a number of university courses, including those in the psychology of motivation, feeling, and emotion, in the psychology of death, dying, and lethal behavior, and in the psychology of myth, magic, and religious experience—and always to good effect.

Until recently I have tended to view these procedures primarily as dramatic demonstrations of certain points I was trying to make about the constructive aspects of conscious experience. Some of the obvious similarities between the experiences reported by participants in my procedures and those reported in the recent literature on LADEs has, however, suggested the possibility of using these procedures as the basis of a more controlled experimental investigation into OBEs in general.

The remainder of this chapter consists of three main sections. The first describes the general methods and procedures themselves. The second describes the results of a recently completed study of the effectiveness of these procedures in producing the intended results. The final section discusses a general theoretical model for the relationship between perception and imagination in producing OBEs.

## General Methods and Procedures

The procedure that follows is presented to prospective participants as a "trip into outer space." The core of this procedure is a set of instructions delivered orally by the "tour guide" to the participants. Before describing these instructions however it is useful to have some picture of the typical physical setting in which these procedures have been administered and the typical psychological set of the participants prior to the initiation of the procedures.

### Physical Setting

The effect of these instructions appears to be equally effective over a wide range of variations in physical setting. In the early years, when I was working with encounter groups, I had the participants recline on the floor, dimmed the lights, and so forth. In later years, when I employed the same instructions in university classrooms, students were seated in hard, straight-backed, wooden deskchairs or amphitheater seats. Often it was not possible to dim the lights. Occasionally we were in rooms in which the need for adequate ventilation precluded the closing of the windows, so that street noises were constantly present. As far as I could tell, none of these variables seemed to have significantly reduced either the proportion of participants reporting the effect or the intensity of the effect the participants reported.

*Psychological Set*

More important than the physical setting appears to be the psychological set of the participants. In both the encounter group and the classroom settings, these procedures have been introduced only after a period of time during which a great deal of open discussion, back-and-forth interchange between myself and the class, and a general atmosphere of low anxiety and mutual trust has been established (in the encounter group after several days and in the classroom after several weeks). Furthermore, in each setting these procedures have been introduced at some point in the broader context at which this particular experience seemed to serve some larger heuristic, didactic, or therapeutic purpose. Most often it has been introduced in the context of a more extended general discussion of the fundamental nature of the processes underlying the psychological defense of projection (see below). Thus, the focus has always been not on the "weirdness" of the experience but rather on its total and complete "naturalness"—on the fact that each individual's capacity to do what we were about to do is but one aspect of the general capacity of human beings to actively "construct" experience from the data we are given at the moment.

*Participants*

Participants have been men and women of all ages from nineteen years old on up through the sixties. The encounter group participants tended for the most part to be business and professional people. The classroom groups, on the other hand, were drawn from the student body of a large urban-industrial public university. They have tended to include individuals from a wide variety of ethnic and economic backgrounds, as well as a wide range of psychological and educational sophistication (see the section on the Evaluative Study, below).

## Instructions
*Purpose*

These instructions are intended to induce in the listener a point of view from which the world-as-experienced is seen in part as *constructed* by consciousness and not merely given to consciousness. In order to achieve this goal I proceed in several steps. I start with certain physical and physiological facts concerning the process by which "objective" experience—the experience of the world "out there"—is created. I then proceed to extend the same line of reasoning to the perception of the "self-as-body"—the so-called body image of the observer; and, finally, to the contents of consciousness itself.

This entire process is done at first on a highly intellectual level. Next I carry the participants through a series of phenomenological experiences in which in actual fact first the world *experienced as* "out there" and then the world *experienced as* "contents of consciousness" are dissolved, so that all that remains is the *experience of* "pure consciousness," with no experienced contents whatsoever. It is this latter state that appears to be formally most analogous to, but markedly less intense than, that reported in the "astral projection," the life-after-death, and the enlightenment literatures, respectively.

*Form of Delivery*

The instructions that follow are delivered slowly in a soft, quiet, and very calm tone of voice. Since my own spontaneity seemed an important factor in creating the kind of relaxed and trusting atmosphere that facilitated the achievement of the desired effect, I never read the instructions. Rather, I keep the main points in mind and let the flow of the moment determine the particular verbal form in which these contents emerge.

*Transcription of the Present Set of Instructions*

After I was asked to write the present chapter I had one such spontaneously delivered set of instructions recorded on a tape recorder. I edited a typed transcript of that recording for readability and literacy. Headings, subheadings, ellipses, and commentary have been added in order to guide the reader through the logical flow of the main points.

As noted above, this particular set of instructions was introduced in the context of a consideration of the general psychological processes underlying the psychological defense of "projection."

[Projection]
So far we have considered the notion of "projection" only as a so-called defense mechanism in the psychoanalytic sense. The mechanisms underlying the process of the projection are, however, among the fundamental mechanisms which govern the nature of human consciousness. So I would like to spend more time with you considering the nature of the mechanism of projection itself in some detail.

[Definition of projection]
For definitional purposes we can say that *projection* is that act by which we take the images which are in our minds and put them out into the world and then act as though they existed out there independently of any acts of our own.

[Projective nature of visual experience]
In order to understand how deeply ingrained this mechanism is in the very nature of human consciousness, let's begin by considering in some detail the nature of ordinary everyday visual experience.

I'd like you to begin by looking around the room briefly, taking in everything that you can see through your eyes.

Now look up here. How far away is this wall from you? Somewhere between ten and forty feet—depending upon where you're sitting in this room. The ceiling is about fifteen feet away, wouldn't you say?

You experience all of those things as existing "away" from you. However, that "awayness" poses a paradox—for if they were really "away" from you, how could you ever see them? Where does that visual image that you are experiencing actually exist? Where is the "thing" that you are "seeing" actually located?

## Explicitly Sensory Component of the Experienced Visual Image

At this point I introduce a somewhat detailed description of the nature of the proximal (retinal) image from which visually projected experiences are most often constructed. I emphasize the fact that this proximal data is nothing more than a two-dimensional curved image, about one-quarter of an inch in diameter, that is partially blurred because of the continual small movements of the eye within the head and continually in flux because of the large movements of the head itself. Finally, I point out that we have two such images that are slightly out of "register' with each other because of binocular disparity. In this discussion I try to be as concrete, vivid, and specific as I can, referring frequently to the listeners' own everyday experiences. I then conclude with the following statement.

> To summarize then: The information which you have directly and immediately available to you from the light entering your two eyes from this room itself is the following: a pair of inverted, two-dimensional, curved images about one-quarter of an inch in diameter, which are always blurred and almost continually changing. This is the *only visual* information which the room itself gives you as you look at it. And it is out of this information (in part) that *you construct* "this room" which is, let us say, a 20 x 40 x 15 foot hollow rectangular prism, sharply focused, and highly stable in its configuration, and filled with objects and people, all of which is experienced as being "out there" independent of you.
>
> Do you understand? *You* construct the room which *you* see. This is not occult mysticism. This is physiological fact.* Now you may be asking: Does he mean that there is *nothing* "out there"? That I myself *build* this room? No. You and I did not construct the "physical" room out there. Carpenters, masons, and so forth, constructed *that* room. What we each construct everytime we look at that room is our *experience* of it. But that is all that we can ever know of "that" room "directly." Do you understand? We are each taking these little patterns of light and *making* out of them our *experience* of this room as a single entity independent of us out there in space. We are making this room. Continuously. And that is an incredible thing. To construct that room from this little bit of light.

This first section of the instructions seems to serve at least three functions. First, it tends to undermine the naïve realism that many participants bring to such an experience; thus it "softens" each participant's defenses against the OBE itself. Second, it does so on "intellectual" grounds—by means of those very same logical and scientific grounds that are usually used to deprecate OBEs. Third, it begins to give each participant a sense that it is possible to accept responsibility for and exercise some degree of control over one's own experiences—*as one experiences* them.

*The theoretical and empirical bases for this assertion are discussed in the final section of this chapter.

*Nonvisual Sensory Component of the Experienced Visual Image*

The next section of the instructions is designed to give participants some sense that the nature of the projected visual image does not depend solely on incoming visual (light) information. Rather, the form of that experience is to a large extent shaped by implicit assumptions about a variety of other sensory properties—both qualities and quantities—that we "read into" that image. I begin this section as follows:

> Now that visual image is not constructed from just light information alone. There is not enough information in the form of the light coming into my eye from the outside to account for the richness and complexity of my experience of the room out there. I must add other information to that construction as well.
>
> What, for example, is implied by saying that the wall is "twenty feet away"? Certainly I "see" it as about twenty feet away. But in that "seeing" is a kinesthetic sense I have that it would take me about five to seven paces before I would reach the wall. If a wall "looked" that far away but I could reach it in one or two paces, for example, I would suspect that one of two things happened: either that someone was playing a visual trick on me or that some system in my brain was malfunctioning. There is no way in my experience that a wall can both look like that wall looks and also be only two of my steps away from me.
>
> Implicit in my visual projection of the image of this room is not just kinesthetic information, but all of the other types of sensory information—auditory, tactile, olfactory, etc., as well.

I then go on to give some concrete examples of how expectations based on both theoretical knowledge and personal past experience derived from *all* our senses—not just our sense of vision alone—often play a major role in the way in which we construct present visual experiences.

> Thus, in the construction of the projected visual image I utilize not only the constraints imposed upon me by the information contained in the "raw" pattern of light projected in the world "out there" into my retina, but also an elaborate set of constraints imposed upon me by the cognitively stored information projected by me from my storehouse of past experiences into each present moment in which the act of construction is actually taking place.

This second section of the instructions appears to serve two functions. First, it attunes participants to the fact that in the OBE that
follows past knowledge and past experience will also play a major
role in the forms that present experience assumes. Second, awareness of this similarity between the OBE and ordinary perceptual
experience reduces the tendency for participants to assume an intel-
lectually critical detachment from the experience itself, and hence
facilitates a deeper subsequent OBE.

### "Having" vs. "Judging" and Experience

Since we all play such a major role in constructing our own personal
experiences, the question that naturally arises at this point is how
we tell "reality" from "illusion," "hallucination," "delusion," and
so forth. I, therefore, next address myself to the appropriate role of
consensual validation in the evaluation of personal experiences. The
key point made here is the following:

> Discrepancies between our perception of reality and other peoples' per-
> ceptions of reality happen to all of us all of the time. It is important to
> keep clearly in mind, therefore, the difference between the *having* of an
> experience and the *judgment* of that experience. Let us say, for example,
> that I report having the experience of seeing a man sitting there in that
> chair [I point to an empty chair] and you do not. Now either I do or do
> not have that experience as I described it to you. If I have had it then I
> have; and if I haven't then I haven't. There is nothing that you or
> anyone else can say that can change that immediately and primarily
> given fact. That is a primary datum of my experience. The fact that you
> have or have not seen the same thing as I have can neither give me the
> experience if I haven't had it nor take it away from me if I have had it.
> And only I am capable of knowing whether or not I have actually had it.
>    Now, it is not that I don't "care" whether you have seen the same
> thing which I have seen or not. I do care. For our common perceptions
> of reality is one of the things we share in common. The point however is
> this: While what you say about what I report can affect my judgment of
> the appropriate category or status to which to assign that experience it
> cannot effect the experience of "having had" that experience itself.

I follow this with some concrete examples of the phenomenological reality of the hallucinatory experience despite its lack of consensual validation and conclude with the following statement:

> In the space trip which we will be taking shortly each of you will have
> a somewhat different experience—depending upon what kinds of spe-
> cialized knowledge and personal past experience you bring to this par-
> ticular occasion. The fact that your experiences will differ from each
> other in no way invalidates the *having* of the experience itself, but only
> the category of experience to which you assign that particular experi-
> ence. The having of it will be whatever it is for you. That is primary.
> That is yours.

The main point of the introductory phase of these instructions is
to leave each participant with the sense that (1) we do in fact construct our experiences—our visual as well as our other sensory experiences; (2) we don't construct that experience out of nothing—
there are constraints on what we construct; (3) some of those constraints are contributed by the physical properties of the objects
themselves as they are out there—some, but not all; and (4) some of
the constraints are supplied by the interplay of our own various
senses, our own past experience, and our need to make the total
body of our experiences coherent. This latter constraint prevents me
from constructing and projecting images in the present that are too
discrepant from my past experience.

*Body Image as a Projected Experience*

At this point I pause for participants to raise doubts and ask specific questions about the material covered so far. I proceed to
answer questions and reassure "doubters" until everyone seems
satisfied enough to be willing to go on. I then proceed as follows:

> If you believe what I have been saying—that you are the creator of your
> experience of the world out there—then it must follow directly that you
> are also the creator of your own body—as you experience it. Most of us
> think most of the time of our minds as a creation—and epiphenome-
> non—of our body, of our brain. That our "minds" are located in our
> brain. What I am proposing to you here and now is that it is equally as
> tenable to propose that our bodies—as we experience them—are the
> creations of our minds, the results of the same type of acts of construc-
> tion and projection by which we create the rest of the world "out there"
> as well. I therefore want to demonstrate to you next that your conscious-
> ness, as you experience it, is not located merely in your head, or your
> brain, as you previously may have thought, but is a mobile tool which

can be moved to any place in your body you wish to move it, and even, as we shall see subsequently, outside of your body entirely.

## Motility of Consciousness

What follows next is a very long, very slow, more or less "standard" relaxation exercise. Participants are instructed to put away all books and papers, to lower their eyelids in a comfortable and relaxed manner, and to assume some position in which they can sit without moving "for about the next twenty minutes." If possible the lights are dimmed at this point, the window shades lowered, and so forth. Total darkness is, of course, *un*desirable, since it facilitates drowsiness rather than relaxed alertness. When everyone has quieted down I proceed as follows:

> Now, I will give you some instructions which will allow you to move your consciousness to any place in your body that you want. The purpose of this is to give you some concrete sense that your consciousness is a tool which can be moved about in your body, and is not merely an epiphenomenon of that body itself. Your consciousness is mobile: It is not located in your head, your stomach, or anywhere else in particular, and, therefore, you can become master of your consciousness and move it to any place in your body you wish. Let us begin.
>
> I am going to talk to you about different parts of your body. As I talk to you about each part of your body I don't want you to *move* that part of your body but only to become *conscious* of it. I want you to do it all with your *mind*. All I want you to move throughout all of the remainder of this exercise is your mind. Everything else is to remain as quiet and as unmoving as possible. Let me ask you again to get comfortable, and then to try not to move—especially because your movement may disturb your neighbor's concentration.
>
> I want you to start by becoming conscious of your big toe. I want you to try to put all of your consciousness into your big toe—so that your big toe is all you are conscious of. Become aware of the shape of your toe. The toenail of your toe. The part of your toe that rests against the adjacent toe. You can feel how your toe rests against your shoe and your sock with your mind.
>
> When you have finished exploring your big toe—with your mind—proceed to explore each of the remaining toes—the second, third, fourth, and little toes—each in the same manner.
>
> When you have done that, then I want you to grasp—with your mind alone—the set of all five toes at once, as a group, without moving any

part of your body, but only your mind. If you feel any residual pain, tension, discomfort, or other sensation, focus upon it, concentrate it, and then let it go.

Now focus upon all five toes at once and study—with your mind alone—how those toes are attached to your foot.

The instructions proceed in this manner throughout the entire body in an orderly progression from the tip of the toes up to the top of the head.

Throughout this procedure several formulas of verbal expression are repeated periodically as seems appropriate. These are:

(1) As each part of the body that is likely to be a locus of tension is mentioned, the participants are reminded: "If you feel any tension, pain, or discomfort, concentrate on it, exaggerate it, and let it go."

(2) Throughout the abdominal and thoracic regions participants are encouraged to explore with the mind's eye and to massage with the mind's hand such hard-to-get-at parts of the body as the colon, the inside of the stomach, and the discs between adjacent vertebrae, and so forth. A similar procedure is used at certain crucial joints, such as the knee joint, the shoulder joint, and the joint at the base of the skull.

(3) In order to counteract the fragmenting effects that focusing on one bodily part at a time tends to have on the unity of the body image as a whole, the participants are periodically instructed to grasp with their minds the "wholeness" of all those parts of the body already mentioned. After everyone "travels through" the entire leg from the tip of the toes through the hip joint, I might say, for example, "Now experience your leg as a whole. Scan it. If there is any residual pain, tension, or discomfort, focus on it—and let it go."

This part of the procedure always ends with the following statement:

And now I want you to experience the totality of your entire *body as a whole*. With your mind's eye grasp the unity of your body as a whole. Scan that body. If there are still any residual tensions, pains, or discomforts, concentrate on them, massage them if you wish, and then let them go.

Finally, I have found it useful in my role as tour guide to go through the entire experience myself as I am describing it to the participants. This helps me to pace the rate at which to move from one location to another, as well as reminds me of those areas in which tension tends to be located and in which exploration with either the mind's hand or the mind's eye might be particularly useful.

## A Trip through Outer Space: The OBE Itself

Having mastered to some degree the mobility of their own consciousness, and having relaxed a good deal of their bodily tension, the participants are now ready for the OBE itself. I have come to call this part of the experience "A Trip through Outer Space." The instructions for this part of the exercise go like this:

> Now what I want you to do is this: I want you to leave your body through the top of your head and stand behind yourself in this room and see yourself sitting there in that chair where you are sitting right now. See how you sit. Look at the shape of your body, the slouch of your body, as you are sitting there. Just see yourself as you are.
>
> Then look around this room, as you know it to be. Look at some of the other people sitting next to you in the room, at the walls, the ceiling, and so forth.
>
> When you have done that, then I would like you to walk out of this room, through the door, and into the hallway as you know it to be out there. [Pause.] Then I would like you to walk down the hallway as you usually do after class and out the exit of the building by which you usually leave this building. Down the stairs and out the door into the street. [Pause.] Go out into the street as you know it to be out there, with all of its sounds, colors, smells, textures, and so forth.
>
> Now I'm going to ask you to do something which you have probably never done before. I want you to start rising up off the ground. Straight up. And as you rise up I want you to look around and see this building we are in right now, and the other buildings which are close to it—State Hall, Science Hall. . . . [I name some specific buildings in the area.] You should be up about fifty feet off the ground right now.

And then I want you to go even higher, so you can see the whole campus, as you know it to be.

And now I want you to rise even further, so that you can see where this campus is located in this city of Detroit—at the intersection of the Lodge and the Ford Freeways—and where the city of Detroit is located in the surrounding areas: Lake St. Clair, the Detroit River. . . . [I name several well-known landmarks that can serve as orienting and reference points.]

Keep rising. You have to move a lot faster now because we are going to have to cover a great deal of distance in a very short time. Now, as you are rising faster and faster I want you to look down and see Lake Erie and Lake Huron. And now you can see the entire state of Michigan. The city of Detroit is rapidly fading now—but the mitten shape of Michigan is quite pleasing with those great bodies of surrounding water—Lake Michigan, Lake Superior, Lake Huron, and Lake Erie.

As you continue to rise faster and faster, you will begin to see the curvature of the earth quite clearly, so that when you are about 200 miles up you can see all of the United States with the oceans on either side and the great Canadian tundra to the north: James Bay, Hudson's Bay, and even part of the Arctic ice cap now.

If you move fast enough and far enough out now you will see the whole blue-green ball of the earth itself now with its swirls of white clouds here and there. A blue-green ball on a black velvet background.

I want you to rise rapidly toward the moon now so that the moon is over your right shoulder. If you look over your right shoulder you will see that the moon looks crystalline-white like a large, pitted mothball—also against a black velvet background.

Keep moving out past the moon now—farther and farther and faster and faster—until both earth and moon shrink to small dots of light on the black velvet background, the larger one blue-green, the smaller one bright white. If you look to your right you'll see the sun—a bright yellow-orange disc—immensely larger than those two dots. The sun, too, is on a black velvet background. To the left of the earth-moon pair you'll see an equally small brick red dot. That, of course, is Mars. And as you rise still farther the other planets of our solar system come into view and then shrink until the entire solar system itself with the sun and all of the surrounding planets blend with the millions and millions of tiny bright dots which make up this region of our galaxy—the Milky Way.

And if you then move up still farther and still faster, you will actually get out of our galaxy and see the whole of the galaxy as it really is, as a spiral nebula, with our whole solar system just one tiny dot in the middle of one arm of that galaxy against a background, finally, of innumerable such galaxies which are everywhere on this black velvet background.

And now—if you go farther, and still farther, out into the blackness itself, these dots themselves will get smaller and smaller, until they themselves fade into the blackness, so that all that remains is that total black velvet blackness itself.

And now, if you go just one step farther than that, you will get to that point at which not even the blackness itself exists. Where *nothing at all* exists. This is the Void. Experience it for a while. See what it feels like to you. [Long pause in here.]

In the early years I would end the exercise at this point. This frequently turned out to be very unsatisfactory from the participants' point of view. Many reported having trouble "finding their way back." Others reported anger and frustration at being left "hanging out there like that" with no easy way to return. In recent years, therefore, I have always guided all participants back through the return trip to earth. The instructions for the return go like this:

Now it is time to begin our trip back to earth. I would like you to start the return by creating for yourself out of absolute nothingness the absolute blackness. And then begin to create those millions upon millions of stars which populate the blackness. Now, among those millions of stars pick out that spiral nebula which is our galaxy—the Milky Way. Now find the arm of that galaxy which has our sun in it. Now head toward the sun.

The return trip is done more rapidly than the trip out, but each reference point used in orienting the person on the way out is mentioned briefly on the return trip. In particular, the participants are instructed to locate each reference point in *their* own field of vision before moving toward it, so that at no point is there a feeling of being "lost out there." The instructions for the return end as follows:

And then find the campus of this university. And then this building on the campus. Now, this time, instead of entering through the door I want you to come right in through the roof of the building. Right through the roof of this building, into this room, and stand once again behind your chair, and see yourself sitting there as you are right now. Look around you at the others sitting there to your left and to your right—with your mind's eye now, not with your body.

And now, when you are ready, in your own good time, reenter your body through the top of your skull. Don't enter your body all at once.

Enter slowly. Fill your body with your consciousness now just as you would fill a glove with your hand. And when you are ready, give a good stretch just as you might when you are waking up in the morning, since it is through this act of stretching that we do in fact fill our body with our consciousness.

And when your body has been filled with your consciousness, from the tips of your fingers and toes all the way to the top of your head, then in your own good time, and very slowly, open your eyes and reenter this room.

After an appropriate length of time the lights are gradually put on, the window shades lifted, and the debriefing session is begun.

Except as noted in the following section below, the debriefing session consists of an open classroom discussion in which all the participants are asked, but are not required, to share with the group "what your experience was like." Participants are encouraged to share both the pleasant and unpleasant aspects of the experience, as well as to discuss whether or not they even had any significant experience at all as a result of these instructions.

## The Evaluative Study

Until I was invited to write this chapter I have always used the debriefing procedures described above as an informal means for evaluating the effectiveness of these procedures and as the basis for making improvements where they seemed necessary. In the early years of using the technique, for example, I would instruct participants to raise a hand if they felt frightened or in any other way needed help. However, a number of participants remarked that after they had left their body and were out in outer space, they went to raise their hand and realized that they could not find their hand. I subsequently omitted that portion of the original instructions. Or again, as I have noted above, I previously ended the trip while the participants were still "out in the white light," assuming that they would just find their way back by themselves. The distress this caused a number of participants resulted in the institution of the "round trip" procedure, in place of the previous "one-way ticket."

After being invited to contribute this chapter, however, I undertook a more objective assessment of the effectiveness of this technique itself. This section reports the results of my investigation.

## Empirical Questions

Three empirical questions in particular were of interest at this stage of investigation.

(1) How *deeply* did participants get involved in the OBE? How far were they able to travel out into space?

(2) How *pleasant* (or unpleasant) was the experience?

(3) Was it possible to identify some of the factors that contributed to the depth and pleasantness of the experience? Two kinds of factors were of immediate interest: Those relating to demographic variables and those relating to previous exposure to either abstract concepts or concrete experiences of this kind.

Data collection proceeded in three steps: (1) a brief written immediate self-report; (2) a standardized questionnaire; and (3) a detailed, written, delayed self-report.

## Immediately Written Report

As soon as all the participants had opened their eyes and appeared to have fully returned to their bodies, they were asked to "write out as quickly and as briefly as you can what that experience was like for you." No other instructions were given.

## Standardized Questionnaire

When everyone had finished writing this brief report, the standardized questionnaire was distributed. The items on this questionnaire, which are reproduced in the left-hand portion of Table 7-1 in the order in which they were given, was hectographed on one side of an 8½ × 11 inch sheet of white paper. Respondents were asked not to identify themselves other than give age, gender, and academic major as indicated. Responses to Question 5 were indicated by a mark on a linear scale containing two anchoring points ("very pleasant" and "very unpleasant"), a midpoint ("neutral"), and seven subdivisions (as, for example, in a standard semantic differential). This scale has been omitted from Table 7-1. Responses to Question 4 were indicated by a checkmark in the blank to the left of each response choice. These blanks, too, have been omitted. Finally, responses to the remaining questions were written into blank spaces following each.

## Delayed Written Report

After the questionnaire was completed, it and the immediate reports were collected. Participants were then asked to "write at home a more detailed report of anything else you can remember about the experience, as well as any comment or suggestions you might have." These reports were collected at the beginning of the next class session, about forty-eight hours later.

## Debriefing

The usual debriefing (described above) was carried out, only this time it was delayed forty-eight hours until the full report had been handed in.

## Participants and Setting

The participants in this study were the students enrolled in an undergraduate course in psychology of motivation, feeling, and emotions at Wayne State University. The procedures were conducted in an ordinary classroom setting as one part of the instructional techniques that I usually used in such classes. This particular class was held in a very old (circa 1880) building, so that lighting and ventilation were poor and the room tended to be overheated even with the windows open. (One participant subsequently noted that the overheating interfered with her concentration.)

*Informed consent.* Students were told one class session in advance that they would be taking a space trip during the next class session, and that those who did not wish to participate in this experience could either miss class that day or come to class but not participate. In either case there would be no penalty for not participating nor would there be any extrinsic reward for doing so. The general atmosphere of the class was such that I believe students accepted these statements at face value. At the beginning of the actual procedures, students were again specifically instructed that at any point they wished they could stop participating. The only request I made was that in that case if possible they sit quietly in their seats so as not to disturb the others.

*Instructions*

The instructions given in the section "General Methods and Procedures" are an edited version of the actual instructions used in the administration of this particular OBE procedure.

# Results

The quantitative results derived from the standardized questionnaire will be considered first; then the qualitative results derived from the written comments and self-reports will be summarized.

*Questionnaire: Quantitative Results*

Table 7-1 summarizes the quantitative results derived from participants' responses to the standardized questionnaire. The left-hand column shows the actual questions and the response categories. The two right-hand columns show the number and percentage of participants giving each response choice to each question. Forty-five students took part in the study.

*Demographic variables.* Table 7-1 shows that 67 percent of the participants were between nineteen and twenty-three years old—the normative range for an undergraduate university class. Those who were above twenty-three years ranged in age from twenty-four through forty-two years of age, with a median of thirty-five years. Forty-five percent of this sample was male, and 55 percent was female. Finally, 51 percent were psychology majors and 49 percent were majoring in other areas of study. These other areas included such diversity as fashion merchandizing, criminal justice, political science, social work, geology, fine arts, nursing, and so forth. These descriptive results give some sense of the diversity of students in this classroom sample, a diversity that is worthy of note since it is typical for Wayne State University, but may not be typical for many other universities.

*Depth of the induced OBE.* The most interesting variable for evaluating the overall effectiveness of these procedures is the *depth* to which each participant "penetrated into" the experience. The analysis of the responses to Question 4 in Table 7-1 shows that only 2 percent of the participants experienced "no effect at all" from these instructions while 27 percent were able to follow the instructions all the way through their bodies. What is particularly striking, however, is that 60 percent of the participants indicated one of the three remaining response categories, all of which imply some degree of OBE. Fifty-one percent were able to go some distance into outer space, and 11 percent were actually able to experience the final and extreme state that I have referred to as "the white light" (or "grey void").

*Pleasantness of the experience.* The response pattern to Question 5 indicates that 94 percent of the participants found this experience pleasant to some degree; 4 percent found it slightly unpleasant; and only 2 percent (one participant) found it "very unpleasant." Once again these quantitative results were in accord with assessments based upon the debriefing sessions I have conducted over the years. What is particularly striking here, however, is that 72 percent of the participants found the experience quite pleasant to "very pleasant." This is in accord with the fact that over the years many students have come up after the class to ask how they could participate in such an experience again.

*Effects of the demographic variables on depth and pleasantness.* A second set of quantitative questions concerned whether either the depth or the pleasantness of the experience was statistically related to any of the three demographic variables—age, gender, and academic major—on which we had data. It would not have been surprising, for example, to find that it was easier or pleasanter for younger students to surrender to such an experience than for older students; or that psychology majors were more critical of such

Table 7-1

Questionnaire Items and Distribution of Responses

| Questionnaire Items and Response Categories | Distribution of Responses | |
|---|---|---|
| | Frequency | Percent |
| *Demographic data* | | |
| Age | | |
|     19–23 yrs | 30 | 67 |
|     24+ yrs | 15 | 33 |
| Gender | | |
|     Male | 19 | 45 |
|     Female | 23 | 55 |
| Major | | |
|     Psychology | 23 | 51 |
|     Nonpsychology | 22 | 49 |
| | | |
| *Substantive questions* | | |
| 1.  Have you ever participated in any activity like this before? | | |
|         Yes | 15 | 33 |
|         No | 30 | 57 |
| 2.  If "yes" when and where? What was it like? | (a) | (a) |
| 3a. Have you ever belonged to a meditation group? If "yes" please describe. | | |
|         Yes | 2 | 4 |
|         No | 43 | 96 |
| 3b. Was your experience anything like that you had in this class? | (b) | (b) |
| 4.  How deeply did you get into the out-of-body experience? | | |
|         Not at all | 1 | 2 |
|         Part of the way through my body | 12 | 27 |

procedures than nonpsychology students. Depth and pleasantness were, therefore, each tested against each of the demographic variables in a 2 × 2 chi-square. Each of the demographic variables was partitioned as indicated in Table 7-1. The response categories for the depth variable (Question 4) were divided so that those which indicated some OBE (the last three in Table 7-1) constituted one category and those which indicated no OBE were in the other cate-

| Questionnaire Items and Response Categories | Distribution of Responses | |
|---|---|---|
| | Frequency | Percent |
| All the way through my body | 5 | 11 |
| Left my body and stood behind the chair | 4 | 9 |
| Out into space | 18 | 40 |
| Out into the "white light" (or "grey void") | 5 | 11 |
| 5. How would you rate your experience on a scale of pleasant to unpleasant? | | |
| Very unpleasant→ 0.0–0.9 | 1 | 2 |
| 1.0–1.9 | 0 | 0 |
| Neutral → 2.0–2.9 | 2 | 4 |
| 3.0–3.9 | 10 | 22 |
| 4.0–4.9 | 16 | 36 |
| Very pleasant → 5.0–5.9 | 16 | 36 |
| 6. Are you familiar with the literature on life after death, out-of-body experiences, or astral projection? | | |
| Yes | 16 | 38 |
| No | 26 | 62 |
| 7. If "yes," were there any relations between (6) and this experience? Describe. | | |
| Yes | 12 | 75 |
| No | 4 | 25 |
| 8. Please share with me any additional comments you might have on this experience. | | |
| Made comments | 38 | 84 |
| No comments | 7 | 16 |

[a]This question yielded no quantifiable results. Responses are discussed in the text below.
[b]Since only two participants had had such experiences, this second part could not be meaningfully quantified.

gory. The responses on the pleasantness variable (Question 5) were divided so that responses of less than 4.0 (that is, those which indicate a mildly pleasant down through a very unpleasant effect) constituted one category, while those of 4.0 or more (that is, those which indicate quite pleasant to very pleasant effects) constituted the other category.

None of these six chi-square tests indicated the existence of any statistical relationship between these demographic variables and the two dependent variables. Indeed, most of the tests yielded chi-square values of less than 1.0.

*Effects of previous experience on depth and pleasantness.* Three of the questions on the questionnaire were directed toward determining if the participants had had any previous experience of a similar kind, since it seemed possible that previous experience might make it easier for a participant to get into the present experience. Question 1 asked about previous similar experience in general; Question 3 about meditation experience in particular; and Question 6 about familiarity with the literatures on OBEs, LADEs, and astral projection.

Table 7-1 shows that only two of the participants had had any meditation experience. This variable was, therefore, not subjected to further analysis. The existence of a statistical relationship between each of the two remaining experience variables and depth and pleasantness was again evaluated by a 2 × 2 chi-square using the same dichotomizations on the dependent variables. None of these four statistical tests was significant.

*Relationship to other OBEs.* One final question that was investigated was the relationship of this experience to other OBEs reported in the literature. Question 6 in Table 7-1 shows that sixteen participants (38 percent) had at least some familiarity with the OBE, LADE, or astral projection literature. Seventy-five percent of those who indicated such familiarity (twelve of sixteen individuals) indicated that there was some relationship between the present experience and the others they had read about. While the data on the extent of their familiarity with this literature and the nature of the relationship of the present experience to those in the literature were not available from this sample, even a conservative interpretation of these statistics nonetheless indicates that the OBEs produced by this technique are in some ways similar to some of the OBEs reported in this literature.

*Relationship between depth and pleasantness.* Two statistical tests were done on the relationship between depth and pleasantness. The first was again a 2 × 2 chi-square using the same dichotomies that were used in the previous tests. This yielded $X_2 =$

1, $p < .001$. The phi-coefficient of association corresponding to this result was .58, and the contingency coefficient was .50. The strength of these tests indicated the value of computing a product moment correlation between these two variables. This was done by assigning the numerical values 0 through 5 to the six ordered responses to Question 4 and correlating these scores with the rating scale obtained from Question 5. This yielded $r(43) = .77, p < .001$.

## Written Reports Results

I could find no relevant differences in content between the immediately written and the delayed self-reports. Therefore, since the immediate reports were done before the questionnaire was administered, and since there is in addition a sense of "unpremeditated immediacy" about the style of these first reports, the following analysis is based upon them alone.

The contents of these reports were generally in accord with the questionnaire responses reported above. Participants who had indicated on the questionnaire that they had gotten deeply into the OBE and/or had found the overall experience pleasant often vividly expressed that fact in their immediate reports. A 21-year-old male English major, for example, wrote:

> The most vivid moment was that in which I "stood" behind myself and viewed the silent class. The feeling of soaring through space was difficult to achieve, but my imagination was at its height when I was asked to float into nothingness. Returning to my body was not difficult, but I felt a positive relief at my consciousness again being seated within my body.

A 21-year-old female psychology major wrote: "Amazing . . . I never have put my body on like a glove before."

And a 21-year-old female social work student wrote: "Everything was okay until I left my body. It was a very foreign experience and because of this it made it very difficult and took lots of concentration. . . . But I really felt more at ease when my consciousness was able to join its body again."

Finally, another 21-year-old female social work student wrote: "It was a great escape. I really didn't want to come back. Peaceful. Very peaceful."

The one participant who indicated an unpleasant overall experience was a 23-year-old male fine arts major who wrote: "Drowsiness. But it seemed that along with that my limbs became heavy—more and more movement left my body. At first the suggestions made me move those parts suggested, then the movement lessened and I became very still—I felt I did not need to move. My hands started to tingle."

This last example is instructive since it indicates the degree to which participants were affected by these instructions, even when they did not report having been either deeply or pleasantly affected.

There is, however, one curious set of exceptions to the general agreement between the written reports and the questionnaire responses. Five participants who wrote in their immediate reports that they had actually been out in the "white light" (or "grey void") subsequently answered Question 4 by marking some alternative that indicated a less deep OBE: Four marked "out in space" and one marked "part way through my body." The reverse does not appear to have ever occurred: No participant indicated on the questionnaire a deeper OBE than that indicated in the immediate reports.

The origins of this bias are not clear. There is, however, some suggestion in the written reports that some participants were not able to "stand behind the chair" (presumably a "lower-level" OBE) but were able to travel "out into the void" (presumably a higher-level OBE). Since the response format in Question 4 implied a unidirectional linear rank order of responses, this ambiguity in the response choices with respect to the experiences may have resulted in a confusion for some participants about which single choice of "level" most appropriately represented their individual experience.

Whatever the explanation, however, the direction of this bias suggests that the reported 11 percent of the participants (five individuals) making it all the way out into the "white light" may be a very conservative estimate, and that a more accurate estimate might be in the vicinity of 20 percent of the present sample.

The written reports also drew attention to one other aspect of the experience that seems worthy of further inquiry. Although four participants reported "dozing off" or "falling asleep" periodically throughout the experience, three of these reported continuing through the entire experience despite these periodic lapses in attentiveness that they describe as "sleep."

## A General Theoretical Model

One question that is invariably raised by participants during the debriefing portion of the procedures concerns my explanation of the OBE. This question appears to be especially important to those who have a very deep experience. In particular, participants are concerned to know whether I believe that what they experienced is "just imagination" or whether I believe there is "something more" to it.

### The Physiological Basis of Constructed Images

Throughout the instructions for the OBE there was repeated stress placed upon the role that each of us plays in constructing our own experiences. This construction was said to be based on a combination of *both* present input and past experience at every moment in time. In offering this explanation I emphasized that this was not merely some kind of mythical or mystical explanation for perception but a representation of the best and most current psychological data and theoretical thinking on this issue. However, I was unable to suggest any reference that integrated all the relevant empirical and theoretical material in a single, concise presentation. Recently, however, Pribram has published a theory that does just this (Goleman, 1979; Pribram, 1975; Pribram, Nuwer, and Baron, 1974). Taking the modern theory of holography as his "root metaphor," Pribram offers what he has named his *holonomic theory of perception*.

Pribram's holonomic theory is entirely consistent with the theoretical point of view that is at the core of the set of instructions that define the present OBE procedures. It provides an important conceptual linkage between the present methodology and the general theory of perception. The unique feature of Pribram's presentation is the "optical information processing" (that is, holography) analogy.

It is possible to carry the optical analogy considerably farther than Pribram has done and in so doing to extend the domain of its psychological relevance beyond that of ordinary perceptual experience and into that of extraordinary perceptual experiences such as the OBEs reported in the present study. The following model for the relationship between perception and imagination like that of the holographic model is concerned with the role of illumination in the construction of experienced images. It was originally designed (many years ago) as a useful tool for helping participants to understand what I thought was happening in both spontaneously occurring LADEs and "enlightenment" experiences, as well as in deliberately induced OBEs such as those we have described.

*Illumination and Consciousness*

One of the striking characteristics of many OBEs, LADEs, astral projection, and "enlightenment" experiences is the importance of the role that *illumination*—"light" and "vision"—plays in each. St. Paul's conversion by means of a blinding light from heaven epitomizes this aspect of these experiences (Acts, 9).

*Imagination, wisdom, and visual perception.* The concept of "vision" and of "light" as illumination is closely tied to the concepts of "imagination" and "wisdom." The word "imagination" appears to belong to the same conceptual nexus as *"mage"* ≈ "sorcerer" ≈ *"wiz*ard" ≈ *wise* man ≈ man with *"vision"* ≈ *"see*-er."

Pribram (1975) writes:

> Briefly summarizing, the holonomic model of brain function proposes that the brain partakes of both computer and optical [i.e., holographic] brain processes. The brain is like a computer in that information is processed in steps by an organized and organizing set of rules. It differs from current computers in that each step is more extended in space—the brain has considerably more parallel processing capabilities than today's computers. . . . The rules of parallel processing are more akin to those that apply to optical processing . . . i.e., holography. The memory storage is also holographic rather than random as in today's computers. . . . The "deep structure" of the memory store is holographic. . . . (p.174)

Pribram then points out that by contrast to Gibson's (1966) ecological theory of perception in which the environment is directly apprehended by the perceiver,

> the holonomic theory is *constructional*. Images are constructed when input from the inferior temporal cortex (or its analogue in other perceptual systems) activates and organizes the distributed holographic store. *Images are produced and are therefore as much a product of the "information*

*residing" in the organism as they are of "information contained" in the environment.* [emphasis added] (p. 175)

[Observations suggest] that direct perception [as described by Gibson above] is a special case of a more universal experience. When what we perceive is validated through other senses or other knowledge . . . we claim that perception to be veridical. When validation is incomplete, we tend to call the perception an illusion and pursue a search for what physical events may be responsible for the illusion. (p. 180)

Indeed, in the Classical Greek tragedy it is often the "blind man" who like St. Paul is the man of *"vision,"* the *wise* man, the *"seer."** Thus, it seems clear that the *"vision"* that is involved in *"wis*dom" does not come in through the eyes but rather has some other source, some "inner" light that "reflects upon" and "illuminates" consciousness in some new or different way. A *"wizard"* is also a *"magus,"* who is a *"magi*cian" whose art consists in the manipulation of the *"imag*ination," and so forth. Considerations such as these suggest a deep and close relationship between the phenomenon of "illumination" and that of "consciousness" in both perception and in imagination (cf. Brent in press and in prep.).

*"Plane"* of conscious experience. This model conceptualizes each person as possessing a psychological entity that I refer to as the plane of conscious experience (PCE). This plane has three properties, which are formally analogous to those of a transparent visual medium such as a windowpane.

(1) If the source of illumination on the opposite side of the medium from the viewer is more intense than that on the same side as the viewer, then the medium acts as a *transmitter* of images.

(2) If the source on the same side is more intense than the source on the opposite side, then the medium acts as a *reflector* of images.

*While the existence of this conceptual nexus seems quite apparent from contemporary English usage, a search of the etymological literature (Klein, 1966; Murray, Bradley, Cragie, and Onions, 1933; Onions, 1966; Partridge, 1966; Skeat, 1879–1892; *Webster's,* 1971) fails to indicate any common origin for the "mag" of *imagery* and *magus.* While some sources trace *magus* to the Persian name for a priestly class of "sorcerors," the English-language Biblical tradition clearly identifies the "Magi" as "wise men," that is, "visionaries" or "seers." These facts taken together suggest that the common conceptual nexus of this group of terms may have resulted from the convergent evolution of two sets of terms similar in their phonetic and conceptual structure, but of different etymological origins.

(3) Finally, if the sources of illumination on the two sides are about equal in intensity, a superimposed image of somewhat ambiguous location results.

This model is schematically illustrated in Figure 7-1. The individual is viewed as being on one side of the PCE (the inside) and his or her environment on the opposite side (the outside).

The experience of *perception* is then defined by that situation in which the intensity of illumination on the outside is greater than that on the inside, so that transmission (the solid line) occurs; *imagination*, by that situation in which the intensity on the inside is greater than that on the outside, so that reflection (the broken line) occurs.

With respect to visual experience, for example, when we are in a brightly lit environment and our eyes are opened, the intensity of the light coming in from the outside is much greater than the intensity of the "illumination" on the inside, and the plane of consciousness acts as a transmitter of external images, so that visual *perceptions* tend to occur. When, on the other hand, we are in a dark environment or our eyes are closed (in sleep, for example, or in blindness) so that no light comes in from the outside, then the plane of consciousness acts as a reflector of internal images: Images originating in our minds are "illuminated" by our "inner light" and visual *imaginations* tend to occur. Finally, when we are in marginally lit environments (out-of-doors at dusk, for example, or on a moonlit night) in which the intensity of the internal and external sources of illumination are about equal, then the images from the two sources tend to become confounded so that *hallucinations* tend to occur.

*Present study.* The instructions in the present study were specifically designed to gradually dampen various "external" sources of energy—those from the outside visual world as well as those coming in from the participant's own body, kinesthetic feedback, for example. The subsequent articulation of a specific, detailed, and highly vivid set of visual and kinesthetic instructions was designed to then increase the intensity of the inner source so as to create on each participant's plane of conscious experience reflected imagery corresponding to OBEs, LADEs, astral projection, and so forth.

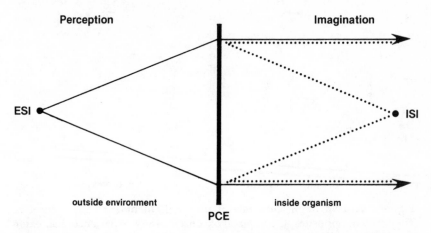

Figure 7-1. A General Model for the Relationship between Perception and Imagination. (*PCE:* plane of consciousness experience; *ESI:* external source of illumination; *ISI:* internal source of illumination; *solid line:* transmitted illumination; *broken line:* reflected illumination).

Since this imagery is a reflection back to each participant of what is already stored in his or her mind, conjured up by the instructions, the tour guide must rely on and exploit knowledge, information, and previous experiences already possessed by the participants.

*Induced vs. Spontaneous OBEs*

In conclusion I would like to use this model to distinguish the processes involved in spontaneously occurring OBEs, such as LADEs and true "enlightenment" experiences, from those involved in induced OBEs, such as those described earlier in this chapter. The literature on the spontaneously occurring experiences suggests that in these experiences the two sources of "illumination"—the inner and the outer—are "momentarily" experienced as but a single source—as One—so that the circuit closes in a manner similar to that shown in Figure 7-2A. The "tunnel" that is "passed through" actually passed the "barrier of distinctions" that previously separated the two sources from each other in consciousness. This barrier is, however, nothing more nor less than the ego itself, in both the psychoanalytic and the Buddhist sense. The breaking through of

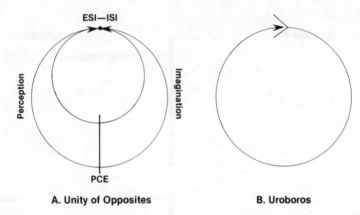

A. Unity of Opposites                    B. Uroboros

Figure 7.2. Two Representations of the "Enlightenment" Experience. A. The unity of opposites. (*PCE:* plane of consciousness experience; *ESI:* external source of illumination; *ISI:* internal source of illumination; *solid line:* unity of transmitted and reflected illumination). B. Uroboros. (A schematic representation of the "hoop snake" that bites or swallows its own tail.)

the barrier by means of the tunnel is analogous to the breaking down of the "insulation barrier" between two adjacent sources of electric current. A short-circuiting of sorts appears to occur. Sometimes, as in the case of St. Paul, the person experiencing the breakthrough is quite literally *blinded* by the intense illumination that accompanies the "short *circuiting*" (that is, shortening of the circuit) of the connection between the inner and outer sources of illumination, as shown in Figure 7-2A. This is sometimes described in the enlightenment literature as the realization of "the oneness of the beginning and the end," "the alpha and omega," that religious mystery which Joseph Campbell (1962) has termed "the secret of the two partners," and which Jung (1944, 1953) has discussed in the context of the Uroburo—the snake that swallows its own tail (see Figure 7-2B).

It appears from this literature as though once one has experienced this union of diametrical opposites, one comes to recognize the union of *all* experience as a multiplicity *within* a Oneness. Through this concretely experienced realization the individual comes to realize that one can start at any point on this perfect circle and look in either direction—"inward" or "outward." When one looks "outward" one sees the world as described by naïve realism and theoretical psychophysics; looking "inward," one sees the world as described by naïve mysticism and analytic psychology. I would like to conclude with a quotation from a Buddhist text known as *The Great Heart (Mind) Sutra.*

> All such things are Mu form, not born, not destroyed.
> Not stained, not pure, without loss, without gain;
> So in Mu there is no form, no feeling, thought, discrimination,
>    perception;
> No eye, ear, nose, tongue, body, mind;
> No color, voice, smell, taste, touch, thing;
> No world of sight . . . no world of consciousness;
> No ignorance and no end to ignorance . . .
> No old age and death, and no end to old age and death;
> No pain, accumulation, destruction, path;
> No wisdom and no gain, no gain and thus . . .
> . . . No hindrance in the mind, no hindrance therefore no fear. . . .
>
>                            (Shimano, n.d.)

## Summary and Conclusions

The principal purpose of this chapter was to describe a technique that has been used over a number of years to deliberately induce OBE's in large groups of naïve individuals in a manner that was pleasant for the participants, required no special settings or equipment, and had no adverse side effects. An evaluative study of the effectiveness of the technique in producing the desired effect was also reported.

The procedure consists of an elaborate set of detailed verbal instructions that are designed to guide the participants through the OBE out into the "white light" (or "grey void") and back again.

The results of the evaluative study indicate that this technique succeeded in inducing self-reported OBEs in at least 60 percent of the forty-five participants in the study, while somewhere between 10 percent and 20 percent of these participants were able to achieve the "white light" state. While the participants in this study were all college students they nevertheless represented a wide range of ages (nineteen to forty-two years old) and of specialized interests and were reasonably balanced between the two sexes. A statistical analysis failed to show any dependency of either the depth or the pleasantness of the OBE upon any of these demographic variables. Thus, these procedures appear to be effective over a fairly wide range of such individual-difference variables. In addition, neither the depth nor the pleasantness of the effect appeared to depend in a statistically significant way upon whether the participants had had past personal experience with or had read about such experiences previously.

All these results suggest, therefore, that this technique might indeed serve as a useful tool for the reliable production of deliberately induced premortem OBEs for the purpose of further experimental investigation.

# References

Brent, S. B., "Motivation, Steady-State, and Structural Development: A General Model of Psychological Homeostasis," *Motivation and Emotion*, 1978, 2, 299–332.

Brent, S. B., *On the Nature and Development of Psychological Structures and Their Functions*. New York: Springer, in press.

Brent, S. B., "Transparency and Meaningfulness" and "The Relationship between Light and Consciousness." In preparation.

Budge, E. A. W., trans. and ed., *The Egyptian Book of the Dead*. New York: Dover, 1967. (Originally published 1895.)

Campbell, J., *The Masks of God*, vol. 2, *Oriental Mythology*. New York: Viking, 1962.

Crookall, R., *Out-of-Body Experiences: A Fourth Analysis*. Secaucus, N.J.: Citadel, 1970.

Evans-Wentz, W. Y., trans. and ed., *The Tibetan Book of the Dead*. 3rd ed. New York: Oxford University Press, 1957.

Goleman, D., "Holographic Memory: Karl Pribram Interviewed," *Psychology Today*, 1979 (February), 9, 71–84.

Jung, C., *Collected Works*, vol. 12, *Psychology and Alchemy*. New York: Pantheon, 1953. (Originally published in German, 1944).

Kapleau, P., *Three Pillars of Zen*. New York: Harper & Row, 1967.

Klein, E., *A Comprehensive Etymological Dictionary of the English Language*. New York: Elsevier, 1966.

Monroe, R., *Journeys Out of Body*. New York: Doubleday, 1973.

Moody, R. A., Jr., *Life After Life*. Covington, Ga.: Mockingbird Books, 1975.

Murray, J. A. H., Bradley, H., Cragie, W. A., and Onions, C. T., *Oxford English Dictionary*, 12 vols. London: Oxford University Press, 1933.

Onions, C. T., ed., *Oxford Dictionary of English Etymology*. London: Oxford University Press, 1966.

Partridge, C., *Origins: A Short Historical Dictionary of Modern English*. 4th ed. London: Routledge & Kegan Paul, 1966.

Pribram, K. H., "Toward a Holonomic Theory of Perception," in Eitel, Kramer, and Stader, eds., *Gestaltheorie in der Moderner Psychologie*. 1975.

Pribram, K. H., Nuwer, M., and Baron, R., "The Holographic Hypothesis of Memory Structure in Brain Function and Perception," in R. C. Atkinson, D. H. Drantz, C. Luce, and P. Suppes, eds., *Contemporary Developments in Mathematical Psychology*. San Francisco: W. H. Freeman, 1974.

Shimano, Eido Tai, ed., *Daily Sutras*. Translation adapted from D. T. Suzuki. New York: Zen Studies Society, n.d.

Skeat, W. W. *An Etymological Dictionary of the English Language*. Rev. ed. London: Oxford University Press, 1879–1882.

*Webster's Third New International Dictionary*. Springfield, Mass.: Merriam, 1971.

# 8

# Communicating with the Dead: An Ongoing Experience as Expressed in Art, Literature, and Song

*Sandra L. Bertman*

*The best philosophical minds have snarled at each other over the centuries in efforts to establish a bedrock definition of reality. If we could all agree on what is "really real," then perhaps it would be easier to answer the core question of this book: Is there "really" communication between the living and the dead?*

*Sandra L. Bertman leaves the metaphysicians snarling in their ancient trenches while she offers instead a guided tour through the social-symbolic sphere of experience. The theme of communication between the living and the dead has often been expressed in art, in literature, and song. Most if not all of us have been influenced by variations of this theme. A humanist educator with particular interests in thanatology and gerontology, Bertman has selected some particularly illuminating examples of this communication from the expressive side of human nature and offers commentary that can stimulate further observation and reflection.*

*This essay does not attempt to fathom what might be behind, beneath, or above the social-symbolic sphere; rather, it provides a valuable opportunity to confront some of the images that have been shaping our thoughts and feelings over the years.*

The dead do not disappear from the lives of the living. They stay connected, and lively communications continue between the two worlds. At times the communication is expressed through a work of art—a painting, an aria, or a poem. Sometimes these contacts are expressed in the symbolic or ritualized form characteristic to a particular culture. Other contacts take a more intimate and personal form, such as a straightforward conversation. Often the contact is signaled by a memory, a dream, or by such an odd object as a piece of clothing, any of which can conjure up phantoms who demand attention. Sometimes the living seek out the dead. At other times the dead seek out the living.

In this chapter, materials selected primarily from literature, painting, and song provide a focus for exploring the connectedness between the living and the dead.

## "So Much Owed by So Many to So Few"[1]

The scene is serene and lovely in John McCrae's poem "In Flanders Field."[2] Delicate red poppies blow gently in the breezes, "and in the sky/The larks, still bravely singing, fly."[2] Evenly spaced crosses mark the graves of the military dead. But don't be fooled: The dead are at rest; but it is not an eternal peace, permanent or nonreversible. The poet induces the dead to reveal their continued concern with the living:

> Take up our quarrel with the foe:
> To you from failing hands we throw
> The torch; be yours to hold it high.
> If ye break faith with us who die,
> We shall not sleep, though poppies grow
> In Flanders fields.

Our intention to keep faith with the battlefield dead and national heroes is expressed through such nationally designated times as Memorial Day, Veterans' Day, Pearl Harbor Day, Martin Luther King Day. We build statues, erect monuments, dedicate buildings, and name streets to honor those who have died in the service of our country's ideals. These honored dead are not consigned to obscurity. Their presence is memorialized to remind us of their relevance. Mark Twain's Huck Finn is totally unimpressed by such heroisms ("But by and by she let out that Moses had been dead a very long time; so then I didn't care no more about him, because I don't take no stock in dead people").[3] As a society, however, we do not forget our heroic dead.

Our culture and history direct us to be guided and inspired by the deeds and examples of dead heros. At times there exists almost a symbiotic need to keep the dead hero alive, or at least to continue to relate to the worshipped one. Fainting, throwing oneself on the tombstone, digging up the grave of a rock singer or movie star, dressing like and adopting the mannerisms of a particular personality suggest such a desperation for attachment.

The plethora of songs to the daring, young, misunderstood rebel, the teen-aged idol of the 1950s, James Dean, is characterized by this active denial. Far from describing him at rest like the dead soldiers in Flanders Fields, the imagery of three songs, "His Name Was Dean," "James Dean, The Greatest of All," and "The Ballad of James Dean,"[4-6] presents the actor's death as merely a scene change. Nothing is really different; the theatre is simply relocated, the substitute director, God ("Great Director did call"[6]), and we, the audience, are replaced by a house composed of celestial beings ("may the angels bid you welcome/as we bid you goodbye"[4]).

The adolescent worshippers console themselves with the promise of continued relationship and interaction. Dean will still be available, as he always was, "acting in [*their*] dreams."[5] Note the use of the present and future tense in their communication to him that no one will ever fill his space:

James *we'll always love* you
*Now* we collect everything we can about you—
Stories, pictures . . . we even bought a record of your life.
*You'll always win* the academy award in our hearts.[5] [emphasis added]

The intention is not just to memorialize by mementos; the promise is more than not to forget; it is to never let go.

In an e. e. cummings poem similar imagery softens the harsh reality of the death of a hero of the Wild West, Buffalo Bill.[7] The word "dead" is never used; the hero is "defunct,"[7] merely out of commission. Like James Dean a legend in his day, this handsome young cowboy and marksman is portrayed as virile and extraordinary in death as he was in life. There is defiant pride in the speaker's question: "and what I want to know is/how do you like your blueeyed boy/Mister Death."[7] But unlike the Dean songs, the poem does not deny the loss. The speaker uses the past tense in eulogizing and reminiscing

> [he] used to
> ride a watersmooth-silver
>                          stallion
> and break onetwothreefourfive pigeonsjustlikethat
>                                              Jesus
> he *was* a handsome man. . . . [emphasis added]

and he directs the communication not to Buffalo Bill but to Death, thus acknowledging the changed reality.

"Love beyond the grave! Love from people you will never meet! Love seeping through paper, parchment and ink!"[9] Erica Jong recalls her amazement at how a remote author—someone she didn't know personally—could penetrate the boundaries of her skin and touch her feelings. As a youngster she believed writers must, indeed, be telepathic. She recalls how she used to "kiss the dustjacket pictures of authors as if they were icons."[9] Unlike Huck Finn, when Jong discovered these writers had been dead for years, she was astonished because she had felt a very personal communication with a (dead) author.

Van Gogh articulated that deeply personal investment and relationship the artist has to his creation. In a letter to his brother Theo, he wrote, "Paintings have a life of their own that derives entirely from the painter's soul."[8] The artistry or work of art becomes a means of self-exposure, the means through which a most intimate inner life is projected outside to a public world.

D. McLean, the composer of "Starry Starry Night,"[10] speaks in song directly to the dead painter Van Gogh. Each refrain returns to the singer's painful awareness of Van Gogh's urgency to communicate his visions ("how you tried to set us free"), of his empathy with the artist's agony ("how you suffered for your sanity"), and of the singer's realization of the distance between the artist and his fellow man ("they would not listen/they did not know how"). Society's rejection of Van Gogh ("for they could not love you") results in his suicide ("you took your life as lovers often do"). But the work of art outlives the man: "Perhaps they'll listen now" cries the voice in "Starry Starry Night."

In "To an American Poet Just Dead,"[11] Richard Wilbur imparts much the same despair about a poet's message unheeded during and after his lifetime. The poet's words failed to rouse the "stupi-fied"[11] suburbanites (the masses who "did not listen"[10] of Van Gogh's day) out of their "sleep of death."[11] Humanity in its "comfy suburbs"[11] is not at all affected by the poet's life, his timeless words, or his demise. Wilbur gives the feeling of grief not to the people but to their cars and appliances, both to bare their real concerns (material possessions) and to underscore how untouched they are:

> For you will deep-freeze units melt and mourn
> For you will Studebakers shred their gears
> And sound from each garage a muted horn?

The dead do "penetrate the boundaries"[9] of some skins. Huck Finn, those who "could not listen,"[10] and the "comfy"[11] suburban-ites, though large in number, are not a unanimity. Living beings, such as Jong, McLean, and Wilbur respond to the dead artists, to their artistry and "messages" and inform them so, directly.

## "Death Ends a Life but It Does Not End a Relationship"[12]

In Hemingway's *A Farewell to Arms* two lovers consider the impact of death on a relationship. Catherine, speaking of a former lover says, "then . . . he was killed and that was the end of it." "I don't know," Frederic says. "Oh, yes," Catherine emphasizes. "That's the end of it."[13]

The idea of death-the-end-of-it has certainly been used to quicken one's partner to consummation of the love act in the here and now. Robert Herrick's "To the Virgins, To Make Much of Time"[14] ("Gather ye rosebuds while ye may") and "Corinna's Going A-Maying"[15] "Then while time serves, and we are but decaying,/Come, my Corinna, come, let's go a-Maying") voice the argument of Andrew Marvell's "To His Coy Mistress"[16]: "The grave's a fine and private place,/But none, I think, do there embrace." Marvell uses the even less genteel imagery of maggots and worms trying his lady's "long preserved virginity" to convince the young mistress of the negative consequences of postponing love-making.

Such literal intimacy with a dead body, denying death-the-end-of-it motivates a Bronte character to dig up a grave, twice, and a Faulkner character to keep a dead lover in bed for years. In *Wuthering Heights*,[17] Heathcliffe digs up and embraces his dear Catherine. In "A Rose for Miss Emily,"[18] death is *the* way of denying the end of a relationship. Emily poisons her lover to keep him from leaving her and to ensure the continuing consummation of their affair until her own death, years later.

But there is also a quest for relationship beyond death. A strong theme in the poetry of Emily Dickinson[19] is a desire for a meaningful union far more than for a physical lust. Dickinson imagines herself lying and talking with her lover in the grave after death. In "The grave my little cottage is,/Where 'keeping house for thee,' "[19] she fantasizes the details of being bonded to her man in the marriage they could never have in life. However, these images of domestic coziness in Paradise are not enough of a healing balm for a hopeless love. The agony of the dilemma "I cannot live with you" or without you in life or in death, is the quiet reality of this pair's communion:

> So We must meet apart—
> You there—I—here
> With just the Door ajar
> That Oceans are—and Prayer
> And that White Sustenance—
> Despair—[19]

John Donne, in "A Valediction: Forbidding Mourning"[20] extols a love so "refined" it transcends the physical ("Careless, eyes, lips, and hands to miss"[20]). It transcends even the possibility of spiritual severance. As phrased by Sara Whitman in a sonnet to an unidentified lover, "death and hell are powerless to divide/Souls whose deep lives lie folded heart in heart."[21] Donne describes the indissoluble union of two souls in terms of a compass—albeit, only one soul with two feet:

> And though it (*one foot or one soul*) in the center sit,
> Yet when the other far doth roam,
> It leans, and hearkens after it,
> And grows erect, as that comes home.[20] [emphasis added]

The union of the lovers is such that the death of one in fact *expands* their boundaries to encompass the dead lover's domain as well.

The dying Robert Jordan in Hemingway's *For Whom the Bell Tolls*,[22] does not view death as expansion, increasing the latitude between lovers as does Donne's lover. Rather, his imagery argues a victory over death in the very words used by Catherine of *Wuthering Heights*[17] when she considers her own demise. She says of Heathcliffe, "If all else perished and *he* remained, I should still continue to be."[17] The love of two beings becomes intensified in its concentration in the one remaining alive. The distance between Robert and Maria ("Rabbit") will, indeed, be *diminished* by his death. As Donne forbids mourning, so Jordan refuses to say goodbye. There is no parting because of death: "Thou wilt go now, Rabbit. But I go with thee. As long as there is one of us there is both of us."[22]

Lovers facing death use such arguments to deny the reality of their impending separation. In *Wuthering Heights*, Catherine, about to give herself in marriage to another man explains to Nelly not only the timeless quality of their love but its incorporation into their very beings. "My love for Heathcliffe resembles the eternal rocks beneath—a source of little visible delight, but necessary . . . I *am* Heathcliffe—he's always, always in my mind—not as a pleasure, any more than I am always a pleasure to myself—but as my own being—so don't talk of our separation again—it is impracticable."[17] Such lovers (Donne's Robert and Maria, Bronte's Heathcliffe and Catherine, Sara Whitman's) would modify Dylan Thomas's conclusion by the addition of a personal pronoun: "Though lovers be lost [*their*] love shall not,/And death shall have no dominion."[23]

The death itself is intended to be the communication in Roy Lichtenstein's painting *Drowning Girl*.[24] The suicide is the last word. The surviving lover will have no chance to respond. The painting offers only the girl's tearstained face and one hand (the only parts of her body not yet submerged by the huge waves) and a cartoonlike caption of her thoughts, "I don't care! I'd rather sink than call Brad for help." The suicide exposes not only unrequited love but the resolute intention to "get at" Brad: now he'll realize the depths of her passion. This act is intended to evoke more than an emotional response of pity or concern; Brad will be punished. The suicide, a spiteful gesture of retaliation, is aimed at saddling the living partner with an albatross—feelings of guilt, inadequacy, and responsibility for the death.

The drowning girl might well have envisioned Brad's response to be that expressed in James Taylor's hit song of the 1970s, written after learning of his Suzanne's suicide. Each stanza of "Fire and Rain"[25] ends with the words of disbelief that he addresses to her, "but I always thought I'd see you again." He relives their conversations as if he is continuing them with her. His body "aches" with the emptiness of his new incompleteness and the realization of their shattered plans ("sweet dreams and flying machines in pieces on the ground"). He even contemplates suicide ("my time is at hand"). Stunned, unable to function, despairing, he asks Jesus "to help [him] make a stand . . . to see [him] through another day."

Recovering after a long convalescence from an illness of such gravity that she thought she might die, Miranda in *Pale Horse, Pale Rider*[26] learns of the death of her lover. Dazed and shocked, she voices her anger at his leaving her: "What do you think I came back for, Adam, to be deceived like this?" She feels his presence, indulges in it, and is loathe to let go: "At once he was there beside her, invisible but urgently present, a ghost but more alive than she was, the last intolerable cheat of her heart; for knowing it was false she still clung to the lie, the unpardonable lie of her bitter desire. She said, 'I love you.' "

Sensing the continued presence of the newly dead is not an infrequent happening for the bereaved. In James Agee's novel *A Death in the Family*,[27] Mary drives all the unpleasant thoughts and imaginings about Jay's sudden death out of her mind by thinking "with such exactness and with such love" of her husband. She *feels* his presence; she even hears his footsteps. "It's Jay," Mary whispered . . . "Jay Darling. Dear heart, can you hear me?" She converses lovingly with her dead husband, assuring him that she and the children will be all right. She tells him not to be troubled or worried and to rest easily. And she asks him to stay near them ("*All you can*").

Mary phrases the need to hold on as reciprocal. Jay wants to be among them, too. The most beautiful expression of this communication with its consolation, love, and ambivalence is Agee's description of Jay's final reappearance:

> When she came through the door of the children's room she could feel his presence as strongly throughout the room as if she had opened a furnace door: the presence of his strength, of virility, of helplessness, and of pure calm. She fell down on her knees in the middle of the floor and whispered, "Jay. My dear. My dear one. You're all right now, darling. You're not troubled any more, are you, my darling? Not any more. Not ever any more, dearest. I can feel how it is with you. I know, my dearest. It's terrible to go. You don't want to. Of *course* you don't. But you've got to. And you know they're going to be all right. Everything is going to be all right, my darling. God take you. God keep you, my own beloved. God make his light shine upon you." And even while she whispered, his presence became faint, and in a moment of terrible dread she cried out "Jay!" and hurried to her daughter's crib. "Stay with me one minute," she whispered, "Just one minute, my dearest"; and in some force he did return; she felt him with her, watching his child.

Mary's father suggests she was hallucinating. Mary yearns and pines* for her lost husband as does another newly bereaved, Lynn Caine (*Widow*),[29] who literally searches for her dead husband in life as well as in her dreams and reveries: "One day when I was on the Fifth Avenue bus I spotted a man who looked like Martin. I pulled the cord and plunged after him. I knew it wasn't Martin, but I tried desperately to catch up with him." This misidentification is only momentary. When Lynn couldn't catch up with "Martin" she felt depressed, "as if Martin rejected me." Perhaps the most painful instance of the power of the illusion and the difficulty of accustom-

*Cf. J. Bowlby and C. M. Parkes on bereavement.[28, 76]

ing herself to the loss is the following account: "When something funny happened, I'd say to myself 'Oh, wait until I tell Martin about this tonight! He'll never believe it.' There were times in my office when I would stretch out my hand to the telephone to call him to chat. Reality always intervened before I dialed that disconnected number."

*All the Way Home,*[30] the film version of Agee's novel *A Death in the Family* ends with a most moving instance of communion and communication. Mary calls on her dead husband ("Oh Jay, Help me!") for help and support as she tries to relate to her son in a way that now incorporates the love of both parents. She accompanies Rufus to his special place, which she'd never visited before ("My this is a nice place. I can see why you and Papa liked to come here"). She talks the uneuphemistic language that Jay had used with his boy. New for her, this language allows for more than form and propriety in her conversation. Mary calls on Jay's strength to be real about the expected baby, no longer the "surprise" from heaven. Also, for the first time, she uses Jay's endearing nickname in addressing Rufus. By so doing, Mary allows the rare tenderness she'd reserved for her husband to be shared with her son, "Come on, goggle eyes, let's go home."

Santayana's sonnet "To W.P. II"[31] expresses the sadness of bereavement, relives memories of shared experiences, and acknowledges an inner emptiness ("With you a part of me hath passed away"). Santayana is confused, depressed, and not sure of the way out of preoccupation. His sonnet is reminiscent of James Taylor's song "Fire and Rain."[25] The concluding couplet of Santayana's sonnet, addressed to his dead love, attests to the continuing power of the bond: "And I scarce know which part may greater be,/What I keep of you, or you rob from me."

The survivor in Taylor's song contemplates suicide as a way out of despair; life without one's love is just not worth living. But, as in Hans Christian Andersen's fairytales,[32, 33] Zefferelli's film *Jesus of Nazareth,*[34] Flannery O'Connor's story "The Lame Shall Enter First,"[35] and Shakespeare's plays,[36, 37] suicide or elective death may also be motivated by the fantasy of reunion. The steadfast tin soldier will be united with his beloved toy ballerina who has preceded him into death,[32] the little match girl with her grandmother,[33] Christ with his father,[34] and Norton with his mother.[35] Cleopatra, placing the asp to her breast, cries out "methinks I hear Anthony call,"[36] and Romeo, thinking his love dead vows to her, "Juliet, I will lie with thee tonight."[37]

Reunion fantasies are not restricted to survivors of suicides nor to those facing imminent death, like Robert Jordan who finds himself talking with his (dead) grandfather.[22] In Sylvia Plath's poem "Daddy,"[38] the speaker confesses to her father "I have always been scared of you." She equates their tortured relationship to that of Nazi and Jew. Even though she must destroy the memory of her father ("Daddy, I have had to kill you"[38]) she nonetheless tries to join him through suicide ("You died before I had time—/Marble-heavy, a bag full of God"[38]).

Heathcliffe's consolation—that which allows him to continue living—is knowledge that he will have Catherine in his arms again. On the evening of Catherine's burial, when Heathcliffe digs up her grave, intending to remove the sole barrier between them ("two yards of loose earth"), he feels her communication, promise, and guidance. As he explains to Nelly, "Her presence was with me; it remained while I refilled the grave, and let me home."[17]

The power of intentionality is most dramatically illustrated by Heathcliffe, who spends seventeen years (and half of a novel's space) attempting to reunite with his dead Catherine. So distracted and destroyed by the separation, Heathcliffe continually communicates with Catherine's ghost whose spirit, he projects, haunts the moors. Ultimately, he will not rest until he overcomes their separateness. Just before his death, he expresses the obsession that so totally devours his existence: "I am swallowed in the anticipation of its fulfillment. . . . You might as well bid a man struggling in the water, rest within arms-length of the shore! I must reach it first, and then I'll rest."[17] Only when he has rejoined Catherine in death can Heathcliffe find peace.

The importance of actual physical union after death—of being buried beside one's love so that their very dust would commingle is expressed when Heathcliffe, having now dug up Catherine's grave a second time and finding her yet undecomposed, exacts a promise of burial beside her from Nelly:

"I disturbed nobody, Nelly . . . and I gave some ease to myself. I shall be a great deal more comfortable now; and you'll have a better chance of keeping me underground, when I get there. . . . I dreamt I was sleeping the last sleep by that sleeper, with my heart stopped and my cheek frozen against hers."

"And if she had been dissolved into earth, or worse, what would you have dreamt of then?" [Nelly asks]

"Of dissolving with her, and being more happy still."[17]

"The Cost Depends on What You Reckon It In"[39] is another instance of such intentionality and readiness to reunite in death. In this story, the administrator of Sherman's Rest Home questions a resident's daughter:

"Who's Sam?"
"Sam is my father," I said. "Why?"
"Your mother wants him. She calls for him."
"He's been dead for twenty-three years," I said.[39]

The context of the conversation is a nursing home long before Mrs. Weissberg's (unexpected) death. Mrs. Weissberg withdraws from the relationships in her living orbit—even the one with her daughter—and fixates on the more meaningful relationship of her life, her husband, Sam. In her loneliness, she calls for him. When confronted with the fact that Sam had died a long time ago, she is incredulous and bursts into tears. Her preoccupation with Sam signals her intentionality—her readiness to rejoin her husband through death. ("She'd been calling his name in her sleep for about two months before Mr. Sherman told me about it.") Her goal is attained when she undergoes a simple operation and dies, much to her physicians' disbelief and surprise.

As in *Wuthering Heights,* the place of burial is not a minor detail of little importance. The promise Heathcliffe exacted from Nelly, Mrs. Weissberg obtained from her daughter. At the cemetery, the mother is buried in the wrong place, that is, not placed beside her husband, Sam, as was her expressed wish. The daughter, having turned her back on acts of abuse during her mother's stay in the nursing home, will not now let such violence occur. Even the rabbi, perhaps unwittingly, allies himself with the system when he says,

"Surely it does not matter where your mother is put to rest. Her soul is already with your father's."[39] The daughter's refusal to have her mother compromised, whatever the inconvenience or awkwardness, is a direct communication of love and understanding to her now dead mother.

A relationship is often continued by the survivor. The living communicate with the dead either to receive comfort, to blame for not being present, or to seek permission to go on with life.

*Momma*, the star of Mel Lazarus's cartoon strip of the same name,[40] seems to be frozen permanently in the anger phase of her grieving. She constantly berates her dead husband, Jerome, for having left her. She must shoulder the family burden and make all the decisions herself: "I'm worrying myself sick . . . but I hope you're enjoying your harp!" In another sequence, Jerome is visualized responding to his wife's communication. He is accused of taking an eternal rest while, as usual, she worries herself sick about the children. (Francis has a new girlfriend of whom Momma does not approve; Marylou might lose her job; Thomas is taking a pay cut and working too hard, etc.) Jerome listens to this recital of worries, interrupting once to say, "That's terrible. That's really terrible." As Momma continues complaining, her deceased mate sighs, "I thought eternal rest meant never having to say, 'that's terrible.' " Momma addresses him sharply: "What was that, Jerome?" "Nothing dear, go on. . . ."

The psychological value of such a communication—of being able to get it all out—is illustrated in George Catlin's painting *Village of the Dead*.[41] An Indian woman is depicted visiting the dried (indicating the passage of time) skull of her husband or child. As Catlin reports:

> seldom passes a day that she does not visit it with a dish of the best cooked food that her lodge affords which she sets before the skull at night and returns for the dish in the morning . . . and she lingers to hold converse and company with the dead . . . sitting or lying by the skull . . . talking to it in the most pleasant and endearing language that she can use . . . and seemingly getting an answer back . . . frequently bringing her needlework with her . . . chatting incessantly with it, while she is garnishing a pair of mocassins.[41]

In the musical *Milk and Honey*,[42] a widow, reminiscent of Catlin's, calls on her dead husband ("Hymn to Hymie") for permission to remarry. Clara asks her late husband, Hymie, to allow her to marry Sol, a new person in her life, should he propose. In their most comfortable and natural language, she converses with him. She cajoles Hymie to "be a sport." Through the communication, permission is granted: "I'm asking Hymie. . . . YES?" In their accustomed idiom, she thanks him, "You're a doll!"

The title of this section, "Death Ends a Life but It Does Not End a Relationship," is open-ended, ambiguous, and incomplete. It is the first half of the opening and closing lines of Robert Anderson's film and play, *I Never Sang for My Father*.[12] The completed statement reads "Death ends a life, but it does not end a relationship, which struggles on in the survivor's mind for some resolution, which it never finds." The author, Robert Anderson, remarried three years after his wife's death. Perhaps a most realistic and sober account of the continued communication between two "bonded" beings is expressed in the conclusion to his moving essay, *Notes of a Survivor*:

> I have been married now for eleven years. It took enormous understanding and generosity on the part of my wife, Teresa, to take me along with my ghosts. We use the Royal Copenhagen porcelain [china bought with his wife, Phyllis, for a future both knew they'd never have]—by her choice we live in the village next to the town where Phyllis and I had our cottage, which now I use as my studio. I have a new life; but though I have a new life, I have an old relationship still struggling in my mind toward some resolution I know it will never find. It has been fifteen years—the struggle still goes on, and I imagine it will go on as long as I live.[43]

## "Have Not Old Writers Said That Dizzy Dreams Can Spring from the Dry Bones of the Dead"[75]

And what of the dead? Are they merely passive, disembodied, disinterested entities who are personified only when their living counterparts need to obtain comfort and support (Julie in *Carousel*,[44] Jay's widow in *All The Way Home*[30]), blame (the *Momma* cartoons[40]), gain permission (Clara in *Milk and Honey*[42]), manipulate (Tevye in *Fiddler on the Roof*[59]), make amends (the daughter in "The Cost

Depends on What You Reckon It In"[39]), reassure oneself of a better life after this one (the black spiritual "Old Black Joe"),[73] or of continued kinship and being "in touch" (Reiff talking to tombstones in the film *Bye Bye Braverman*,[74] the protagonist "loving" the unknown dead in *The Death of a Nobody*[72]). Do they ever take the initiative to make contact? Do they have the same need to find meaning, to explain themselves to themselves? Do they have a need to deliver a message to others?

The dead may have their own "grief work" to do. In the musical *Carousel*,[44] tough and free-spirited Billy married tender Julie, lost his job, learned he was about to become a father, planned a robbery, and killed himself to prevent being captured. After fifteen years of Purgatory, Billy is denied entrance to Heaven until he redeems his soul. He is permitted to return to earth for twenty-four hours during which time he must perform at least one good deed. Catching a glimpse of his unhappy teenage daughter he steals a star to give her as a gift. Awkwardly, when he cannot persuade her to accept the star, he slaps her. But his slap transmits a kiss-like touch rather than a hurt and allows his daughter to feel the love she needs in order to acquire the self-assurance and confidence she lacks. On some level, Julie, too, is aware of the happening and is reassured that she was right to have married Bill after all. Bill's continued support and love is promised ("You'll Never Walk Alone") and the communication is complete when Julie repeats and resings his words.

A most common—and consuming—reason for the dead to initiate reconnection is to avenge a wrong, as the ghost in *Hamlet*,[45] or to right a matter, as the spirits in *A Christmas Carol*.[46] The play opens with the apparition of the Ghost; the novel opens with the lines "Marley was dead, to begin with. There is no doubt whatever about that."[46]

The Ghost speaks directly to Hamlet, explaining his penance and charging him with the task of vengeance for his father's murder:

> I am thy father's spirit,
> Doomed for a certain term to walk the night,
> And for the day confined to fast in fire,
> Till the foul crimes done in my days of nature
> Are burnt and purged away. . . . [45]

Marley's ghost is doing penance for not having "walked amongst his fellow-men" in life. His charge is to have Scrooge avoid the error of his ways: "I wear the chain I forged in life"; "I am here to-night to warn you that you have yet a chance and hope of escaping my fate."[46] The ghost, doubted by Hamlet ("The spirit that I have seen/May be the devil") returns to remind him of the revenge he still must seek ("Do not forget. This visitation/Is but to whet thy almost blunted purpose"). As promised by Marley's ghost, three spirits would visit Scrooge to help him discern how to alter his life. In his last response to a spirit, Scrooge vows to honor Christmas in his heart and try to keep it all the year. Scrooge, formerly ungenerous, unhappy, unkind, and unloved, who, like Marley, had never walked amongst his fellow man, is quite transformed. The novel informs us Scrooge does, indeed, live up to his good intentions: "He had no further intercourse with Spirits, but lived upon the Total-Abstinence Principle ever afterwards; and it was always said of him that he knew how to keep Christmas well, if any man alive possessed the knowledge."[46] The formerly indecisive and rather ineffectual Hamlet does break out of his bind of inaction to right the wrong. He avenges his father's death and, so doing, rid's Denmark of the "something rotten" by which the entire state was contaminated. Hamlet dies in the process ("Now cracks a noble heart"[45]) and is accorded a hero's funeral.

In Jewish literature the dybbuks are the spirits with unfinished business who return to interact with the living. Frequently abrasive, sacrilegious, and brazen, they're sometimes rather irresponsible with their power to see into people's inner souls. They take great delight in exposing the sins and secret desires of the most respected and religious of men, such as Reb Sheftel (in Singer's "The Dead Fiddler"[47]), who is so pious, we are told, that "on the eve of Passover he ordered that the cat wear socklets on its feet, lest it bring into the house the smallest crumb of unleavened bread." When Sheftel asks the dybbuk why he chose to enter his daughter, the dybbuk is less than respectful in his reply: " 'Why not? She's a good-looking girl. I hate the ugly ones—always have, always will.' With that, the dybbuk began to shout ribaldries and obscenities, both in ordinary Yiddish and in musician's slang."[47]

Unlike the frisky, bothersome poltergeists ("racketing spirits"), whose reason for being seems to be mostly mischievous (compare Thurber's *The Night the Ghost Got In*[48]), the dybbuks' hauntings have purpose. These dead spirits don't just take refuge in random bodies. In Singer's "The Dead Fiddler," the dead bridegroom enters his beloved's body to help her prevent the arranged marriage that is a travesty to their love. Reminiscent of the Heathcliffe-Catherine affair, where one feels, indeed, "possessed" by the other person, a physical barrier to wedded union with any other is not enough. Literally, the dybbuk returns to the land of the living to fully claim what is his. Once claimed, his mission is completed.

Reb Sheftel's penance was to complete the remaining unfinished business for the dybbuks, that of proper burial and mourning rites that had somehow not been their lot.

In another Singer story, "Two Corpses Go Dancing,"[49] Itche-Godl returns to haunt his wife (who has remarried) and is allowed to complete, literally and symbolically, the unlived experience that was his life. He is like Billy of *Carousel*, infused with the breath of life for a short time, and suggestive of Marley (*A Christmas Carol*) in having been guilty of being a corpse when alive. Itche-Godl, the "weakling and simpleton . . . (may he rest in peace . . . begging your pardon)," who went unmourned from the world ("the neighbors were too busy to walk behind the hearse, and the body was hurriedly disposed of. Not even a marker was placed over the grave"), becomes famous ("the community erected a tombstone over his grave") honored, and "immortalized" by his (ex-) wife's naming her son after him.

The story is narrated in the first person by a devil who refers to himself as "The Evil One" and admits it always has amused him to play tricks with the dead as well as with the living. But, as with the dybbuks, even the devil's fun is not all that irrelevant. The story ends with the devil speaking directly to the reader, suggesting that Itche-Godl, rather like T. S. Eliot's hollow men, is not such an unusual or alien being: "The world is full of dead ones in sable capes and fur coats who carouse among the living. Maybe your neighbor, maybe your wife, maybe you yourself. . . . Unbutton your shirt. It's possible that underneath your clothes your body is wrapped in a shroud.[49]

Itche-Godl managed to catch the living community up in com-

pleting an unfinished experience of his own; they actively participate in the wedding plans of the two (unknown to them) corpses.
The passion of marriage is never quite consummated in life—like
Bronte's Heathcliffe or Faulkner's Miss Emily—Itche-Godl's new
passion has to do with a woman he never knew when alive. But the
reader is left with the feeling that Itche-Godl's life-in-death is a
bonus; he was more the devil's pawn than ever his own man.

An active intervention of the dead to right a cause takes place in
*Star Wars*[50] when the recently deceased Ben Kenobe, the last keeper
of the Force, speaks to his young protégé, Luke Skywalker, who is
attempting to destroy the spaceship of the Evil Ones. Kenobe directs Luke to shut off his computer and launch the rockets relying
only on the feelings of trust in the Force.

A revenge, as in *Hamlet*, appears maliciously in Pushkin's "The
Queen of Spades."[51] The dead countess visits her "murderer," Hermann, promising forgiveness if he will marry his niece and agree to
cease gambling. But he has one last time at cards and the countess
becomes his advisor: " 'I have come to you against my wish,' she
said in a firm voice. . . . 'Three, seven, ace will win for you if
played in succession, but only on these conditions. . . .' "

Feeling secure in the advice of the dead countess, he is shocked
when he comes up with the wrong card during the final gamble.
Hermann is financially ruined. By turning up a queen rather than
an ace, Hermann senses the countess's revenge: "at [this] moment
it seemed to him the queen of spades winked her eye at him. He
was struck by her remarkable resemblance. . . ." The subsequent
insanity of Hermann, "now confined in room 17 of the Obukhow
Hospital" constantly muttering "Three, seven, ace!" "Three, seven,
queen!" is the ultimate poetic justice.

The dead at times inquire of ongoing life. Within the framework
of a spoken ballad, the dead man in Housman's "Is My Team
Ploughing,"[52] interrogates his living friend about the life he loved,
his land, possessions, and prior relationships. Has this dead man
completed his "grief work"? Is he no longer feeling the pain of
separation when he asks "Is my girl happy/that I *thought* hard to
leave/And has she tired of weeping" [emphasis added]. A continued concern seems evident; feelings of possessiveness and of caring
still exist. Earlier in this verbal exchange, prior to the mention of

the dead man's sweetheart, the living respondent exhibited comfort
and directness in his replies. Now his answers smack of an evasive-
ness, even an urgency to cut off the questions and end the conversation, "Your girl is well contented./Be still, my lad, and sleep."
Perhaps the dead man's agenda is to put this friend in touch with
feelings of guilt or betrayal at being the lover of his girl. The imagery of the concluding stanzas with the puns on "bed" (sleep with,
grave) and "lie easy" (untruth and/or at peace) hint at the truth:

> "Is my friend hearty,
>     Now I am thin and pine,
> And has he found to sleep in
>     A better bed than mine?"

> Yes, lad, I lie easy,
>     I lie as lads would choose;
> I cheer a dead man's sweetheart,
>     Never ask me whose.

In the final act of *Our Town*,[53] Thorton Wilder's setting (a cemetery) and the vantage point of the speakers (actors seated in their
graves) is identical to that in the Housman poem, but unlike in
Housman's ballad, the degree of a dead man's concern is not open
to interpretation. Thorton Wilder depicts his dead as indifferent to
the pains of the living. In the stage directions to *Our Town*, he goes
so far as to specify the posture and speech tones of his actors: They
"do not turn their heads or their eyes to right or left, but they sit in
a quiet without stiffness," and when they deliver their lines the
effect must be "matter-of-fact, without sentimentality and, above
all, without lugubriousness." As the stage manager explains to the
audience, the dead don't stay interested in us living people for very
long: "Gradually, gradually they lose hold of the earth . . . and the
ambitions they had . . . and the pleasures they had . . . and the
things they suffered . . . and the people they loved. They get
weaned away from earth—that's the way I put it, weaned away."[53]

In the final act, Emily dies and joins the dead of her town. In
spite of their advice, she decides to return to earth to relive a day of
her life. Newly dead, that is, not yet "weaned away," the pain of
observing herself relive the day is overwhelming. She sees how

taking-for-granted and matter-of-fact we all are ("Oh Mama, just look at me one minute as though you really saw me . . . LET'S LOOK AT ONE ANOTHER"). She breaks down and, sobbing, asks the stage manager to return her to the cemetery:

> EMILY: I didn't realize. So all that was going on and we never noticed. Take me back—up the hill—to my grave. But first: Wait! One more look. "Good-by, good-by world. Good-by Grover's Corners . . . Mama and Papa. Good-by to clocks ticking . . . and Mama's sundresses and hot baths . . . and sleeping and waking up. Oh earth, you're too wonderful for anybody to realize you." [She looks toward the stage manager and asks abruptly, through her tears] Do any human beings ever realize life while they live it?—every, every minute?
>
> STG. MGR: No. [Pause.] The saints and poets, maybe—they do some.

Emily returned from the dead is unseen by the living. Not so with Lazarus. When Jesus called him by name, "Lazarus, come out," as reported in the New Testament, John 11:44: "The dead man came out, his hands and feet bound with bandages, and his face wrapped with a cloth. Jesus said to them, 'Unbind him, and let him go.' "[54] There was no problem of recognition, no question of identity, no suggestion of trickery or of the imposter.

As a matter of fact, for quite a while no one was aware of anything strange, or even considered the man might be at all different because of his experience of having been dead. In "Lazarus"[55] Leonid Andreyev makes specific mention of this fact. He comments that "for a long time no one noticed in him . . . oddities." Andreyev then goes on to describe not only the physical changes to the man who has returned from the dead, but the personality transformation: "Before his death Lazarus had always been cheerful and carefree, fond of laughter and a merry joke. . . . But now Lazarus had grown grave and taciturn, he never jested, himself, nor responded with laughter to other people's jokes. . . ."[55] Even Lazarus's speech had lost its vitality—not just in terms of tonality (matter-of-fact-like, reminiscent of *Our Town*'s dead), but in terms of profundity and significance: "the words which he uttered, very infrequently, were the plainest, most ordinary and necessary words . . . as those sounds with which animals express pain and pleasure, thirst and hunger. They were the words that one can say all one's life, and yet they give no indication of what pains and gladdens the soul." Lazarus's contact with the living is characterized by passivity and indifference. The three days of his death were enough time to have him "weaned away," as Thorton Wilder's stage manager would have put it.

Is the returned Lazarus any more his own man than Itche-Godl? Mightn't Singer's devil have used Lazarus's sloughed-off skin, the outer covering of a former self, as his "medium" just as well? The Lazarus-the-medium idea is more forcefully suggested by Eugene O'Neill's imagining on the Lazarus theme in his play *Lazarus Laughed.*[56] Lazarus's demeanor, as described in the opening directions, is trancelike, "staring straight before him as if his vision were still fixed beyond life." Totally bewildered and offended by his returned son's behavior, Lazarus's father curses God for sacrilege—for using his son's body as such a container: "I curse the day he called my good son Lazarus from the grave to walk again with a devil inside him! It was not my son who came back but a devil." The chorus, too, notices a significant change. Their words imply almost an emptying out of human feelings before his body was returned to life: "There is no longer any sorrow in his eyes. They must have forgotten sorrow in the grave."

The only instance in which Lazarus markedly alters his gaze, breaks his pattern of laughter as response even to the most humanly defined "tragic" of events, is at his wife's death. He betrays human vulnerability as he holds her body in his arms, soothing her to "Go in peace—to peace." He acknowledges how difficult her life has been, admits to his own loneliness, and pleads with her to signal him when she understands what his life-death-life is all about:

> Lazarus:   (bending down—supplicatingly) Miriam! call back to me! Laugh! (He pauses. A sound of dead silence. Then, with a sound that is very like a sob, he kisses her on the lips) I am lonely![56]

Quite unlike Emily or Bill or even Itche-Godl, Lazarus had no personal agenda—no unfinished business of his own to complete. Even in his role as medium, he is different from Itche-Godl because Lazarus believed in the message he was being used to convey, that there was no death, no loneliness, only eternal life if one believed in Christ. The message he delivers is not so different from Emily's painful revelation, that people become too busy to laugh and love one another, that we living folk actually live by denying life.

## It's Fancying, Fable-making, Nonsense Work"[57] or Is It?

The medium is a middleman, or rather, since the Delphic Oracle, traditionally, a middlewoman. The medium is the means ("Good, bad, indifferent, still the only means/Spirits can speak by," writes Robert Browning in "Mr. Sludge, 'The Medium' "[57] by which the living make contact with their dead. Far earlier than the Pythian Priestess of Greece, as early as 1056 B.C., such beings have been providing service on demand. In the Biblical story, before venturing into battle, King Saul seeks consultation with the "witch" of En-dor.* Saul asks of his servants, "Seek me a woman that divineth by a ghost, that I may go to her and inquire of her" (1 Samuel, 28:15). When such a woman is located, he asks her to "bring up" dead Samuel, which she does: "And Saul perceived that it was Samuel. . . . And Samuel said to Saul: 'Why hast thou disquieted me to bring me up?' "[58]

But mediumism has always been associated with an aura of fraud and chicanery. King Saul visits the lady ("witch") "by night" and in disguise. Indeed, he himself has prohibited such practices ("And Saul had put away those that divined by a ghost or a familiar spirit out of the land.")[58]

In modern times, a most charming example of such chicanery is *Fiddler on the Roof.*[59] Tevye takes advantage of his wife's belief in the retributive powers of the dead to block the arranged marriage of his daughter to the widower butcher. Tevye pretends to be awakened from a bad dream, which his wife, Goldie, offers to interpret ("Tell me what you dreamt/And I'll tell you what it meant"). Recreating the dream in all its ghastly splendor, replete with bodies

*Some later translations of the Old Testament change the word from "witch" to "medium."

rising from their graves, he describes a celebration at which all their beloved departed (most especially Goldie's dear grandmother, Tseitel) happen to be present. Goldie's delighted interpretation: their daughter's wedding to the widower butcher. Much to her surprise (and annoyance), grandmother Tseitel continually congratulates and blesses ("mazel-tov's") the bride and the tailor. Suddenly the festivities are interrupted by the entry of the butcher's late wife, FrumaSara. Angry at the thought of another woman getting her furs and jewels, FrumaSara screams her vindictive wedding present—a union of three weeks followed by death to the bride. The wife's conclusion (and Tevye's chuckle to himself as he blows out the candle and they return to sleep) is that the marriage with the butcher is not meant to be. Furthermore, Goldie concludes, "If my grandmother Tseitel (may she rest in peace) took the trouble to come all the way from the other world to tell me about the tailor . . . all I can say is it must be for the best."

Browning's "Mr. Sludge, 'The Medium' "[57] is a most distasteful sort, who, caught cheating, begs and swears by the soul of the angry, tricked gentleman's dead mother not to be exposed. The poem depicts Sludge eavesdropping at his clients' keyholes, treating his spirit world as a peepshow, and performing himself as a "showman's ape."

Browning's intention is to castigate the medium (alleged to be Mr. Home, whose spirit circles Browning's wife, Elizabeth, evidently visited).

One of the most sensitive accounts of a medium at work is depicted in Singer's story, "The Seance."[60] Set in 1946 in New York, in a heavily draped apartment, with planchette, crystal ball, ouija board and all, the shaman, Mrs. Kopitzky, doubled-chinned with warts, falls into trances and becomes taken over by spirits who speak through her body. Singer suggests contrivance, but far more gently than does Browning. Ventriloquism is hinted at by such a detail as identifiable speech peculiarities: "Baaghaver Krishna began to speak in English with his foreign voice that was half male and half female, duplicating Mrs. Kopitzky's errors in pronounciation and grammar." When trickery is detected in physical phenomena—an apparition is caught changing in the bathroom—the client, Dr. Kalisher, does contemplate the possibility of

ghost hiring; but unlike the irate gentleman who confronts Mr.
Sludge with accusations of swindling, Dr. Kalisher merely
grumbles to himself about such a "crazy—meshugga, a ridiculous
woman."

Unlike Mr. Sludge, Mrs. Kopitzky believes in her ghosts. As she
explains to the somewhat cynical Dr. Kalisher: "There *are* ghosts,
there are. . . . They watch over us from above, they lead us by the
hand, they measure our steps."

But the medium is only half of the seance: The medium exists
because of a willing, believing audience. Dr. Kalisher does not seriously challenge Mrs. Kopitzky. This client, and King Saul, are a far
cry from the credulous believers whose questions at seances are
parodied by James Russell Lowell:

> Could matter ever suffer pain?
> What could take out a cherry-stain?
> Who picked the pocket of Seth Crane,
> Of Waldo precinct, State of Maine?
> Was Sir John Franklin sought in vain?[61]

Though unscrupulous and a braggart, Mr. Sludge is openly disdain-
ful of his audience; he refers to his "guests" as "nuts" and "fools."
Mr. Sludge corroborates what the Lowell burlesque suggests, that
the audience is silly.

But Mrs. Kopitzky is the caring friend to her client. Though ini-
tially Lotte Kopitzky had romantic intentions toward Dr. Kalisher
(of which the spirits, with their "taste for matchmaking," seem to
approve), the interaction becomes one of companionship between
two lonely, disparate beings. Mrs. Kopitzky functions somewhat as
a therapist—knowing her client's needs and helping him live out in
fantasy what was either not enacted in life with Nella or not worked
through during the period of his bereavement. Mrs. Kopitzky accomplishes the consolation (Nella's questionable materialization,
not withstanding) that Dr. Kalisher's dead love is not gone forever.
Dr. Kalisher comes to believe his medium's credo, that "there is no
death. . . . We life forever, and we love forever." Even more extraordinary, Dr. Kalisher can explain his impotence; he no longer
needs to blame it on his prostate condition or on Nella. He can let
the dead Nella go:

". . . how can I bring over Nella when she has already perished? Unless death itself is nothing but a sexual amnesia." He awoke and saw Mrs. Kopitzky bending over him with a pillow which she was about to put behind his head.

"How do you feel?"

"Has Nella left?" he asked, amazed at his own words. He must still be half asleep.[60]

The medium is a flesh and blood vehicle, a connector. In Faulkner's "A Rose for Miss Emily,"[18] the medium is quite literally a "flesh and blood" corpse. That necrophilia was indeed the way Emily communicated with her dead lover and that such a relationship continued over time is implicit in the reported details of the narrator. After the death of Miss Emily, this male corpse was discovered in a locked upstairs bedroom apparently frozen in "an attitude of embrace." The narrator comments on the indentation of a head in the second pillow—"one of us lifted something from it, and leaning forward . . . we saw a long strand of iron-gray hair."[18] Emily's hair was black when her lover died.

But as already seen, the dead may communicate a message directly, without an intermediary. For Peter Ivanovich in *The Death of Ivan Ilych*,[62] the facial expression on the corpse conveys an admonition about living a superficial, unexamined life, and assuming one is immune to death:

> The expression on the face said that what was necessary had been accomplished, and accomplished rightly. Besides this there was in that expression a reproach and a warning to the living. This warning seemed to Peter Ivanovich out of place, or at least not applicable to him. . . . so he hurriedly crossed himself once more and turned and went out the door—too hurriedly and too regardless of propriety, as he himself was aware.

Tombstones also beam their messages, usually terse comments on life. In Master's poem *Spoon River Anthology*,[63] the dead tell their stories through their epitaphs. Those voices, which continually repeat the recognition after death that life had been wasted and is now forever irrecoverable, would probably cause Peter Ivanovich the same discomfort as the inscription on Hannah Sutfin's stone,[64] in Springfield, New Jersey:

> Remember Man, As You Pass By
> As You are now So Once was I
> As I am now So must You be
> Prepare for Death & follow me

But sometimes the message is a personal accusation. In the case of Warren Gibbs, a living sibling (reminiscent of Hamlet's father's ghost) inscribed the tombstone for his brother who died of arsenic poison:

> Think my friends when this you see
> How my wife hath dealt by me
> She in some oysters did prepare
> Some poison for my lot and share . . . .[65]

Another link to the dead is in memory, in dream, or in objects once associated with the person gone. In "Gifts,"[66] the writer, "cold beyond imagining," puts on a sweater of her dead mother's and thinks "it's like having her arms around me." Seeing or touching a piece of clothing of a dead, dear friend can easily elicit memories. In fact, the clothing is worn as an emblem of the communication:

> Shall I say how it is in your clothes?
> A month after your death I wear your blue jacket.
> The dog at the center of my life recognizes
> You've come to visit, he's ecstatic.[67]

A melody,* a mood, or a moment in time can arouse a thought of the dead. "It is strange how the dead leap out at us on street corners, or in dreams," muses a character in Virginia Woolf's novel, *The Waves.*[68] Yeats, too, is well aware of the power of dreams or reveries to bring him near. In "A Deep Sworn Vow"[69] he acknowledges to his lost love:

> . . . when I clamber to the heights of sleep,
> or when I grow excited with wine,
> Suddenly I meet your face.

Despite Tevye's fantasy revelation, the dream is not vulnerable to conscious manipulation. Indeed, it was only because the prophetic

*Cf. "You'll Never Walk Alone," for example, from *Carousel*[44].

vision of Saul's future had not been forthcoming to him in a dream ("the Lord answered him not, neither by dreams, nor by Urim, nor by prophets"[58]) that he sought help from the "witch" of En-dor.

The dream is direct access to a being's most inner feelings and desires. In *My Grandson Lew*,[70] the grandfather who died when Lew was only two reappears to Lew (now six years old) when he is asleep. This happening obviously fulfills the young boy's hidden wish to be together with his grandfather again.

While the dream allows suppressed desires to surface and become intelligible in sleep, oftentimes feelings surface into consciousness without an individual's being at all aware of what he's experiencing. The character in *The Waves* is suddenly stabbed by a feeling before he is able to identify its source:

> Heavens! How they caught me as I left the room, the fangs of that old pain! The desire for someone not there. For whom? I did not know at first; then remembered Percival. I had not thought of him for months. Now to laugh with him, to laugh with him at Neville—that was what I wanted, to walk off arm in arm together laughing. But he was not there. The place was empty.[68]

The pain itself is the vivid embodiment of the memory of the person missed.

As illustrated in *My Grandson Lew*, this intense feeling need not always be negative. Lew's mother acknowledges that there is pleasure in memory as she thanks her son for reviving her father by telling her of his dream, "You made him come back for me tonight by telling me what you remember."[70] She reexperiences long forgotten instances when she shares her remembrances of Lew's infancy with him. While so doing, a new and warm experience, with a life of its own, emerges between mother and child. Mother and child need not be isolated in their missing of grandpa; they can remember him together.

For the poet, memory fuses with words. In "For Johnny Pole on the Forgotten Beach,"[71] Anne Sexton revives her brother in the act of writing. The first stanza accomplishes what shared remembrances did for Lew and his mother, recollections of pleasant childhood memories, in the present tense ("Johnny, your dreams move summers inside my mind"). The horrible, painful images of her brother's lonely death on a beachhead during the war ("Like a bean bag, outflung, head loose/and anonymous he lay") haunt her much the same way as does the enduring pain experienced by the character in *The Waves*. Sexton articulates the need for a repetitive connecting experience: "I think you die again/and live again,/Johnny, each summer that moves inside my mind." The dead are not simply buried. They are not out of mind. They are part of our unfinished business.

## "Dead Man, Dead Man . . . You See That I Have Not Deserted You"[72]

In *The Death of a Nobody*,[72] the protagonist reflects on the reciprocity and reflexiveness of the relationship when he muses about a dead man: "Of course, he's not the only one to be dead. But the thousands of others, mean nothing to me today. It's him I am thinking about, nothing but him. I feel as if I were carrying out his last wishes." "If I were a magician of long ago, I should call up his shadow. I need to see him face to face, and he needs to be called back. What an extraordinary adventure! He is dependent on me, and yet he dominates me."

Be it in symbol, in mind, in memory, or in felt presence, *we*, the living, stay connected to *them*, the dead, and sound our connectedness in language and in heart. The dead do not leave us: they are too powerful, too influential, too meaningful to depart. They give us direction by institutionalizing our history and culture; they clarify our relationship to country and cause. They immortalize our sentiments and visions in poetry, music, and art. The dead come to inform us of tasks yet to be completed, of struggles to be continued, of purposes to be enjoined, of lessons they have learned. We need the dead to release us from obligations, to open new potential, to give us belongingness and strength to continue with our lives.

A richer grasp of such an eternal connectedness and of the solace in this relatedness might help create a more sympathetic attitude toward the pain of loneliness, toward active participation in the comforts of communication with the dead, and toward understanding the driving psychological forces that can dominate a person's

behavior when under the influence of an overwhelming preoccupation. Such a grasp might also be of great help to those dying and to
those losing another—for knowledge of connectedness can serve to
ease the pain for both. As the lore of the humanities constantly
informs us, it really is to our disadvantage to insist that dead is
dead in a logical imperative.


# References

1. W. S. Churchill, Speech, House of Commons, Aug. 20, 1940.

2. J. McCrae, "In Flanders Field," in Off to Arcady, ed. M. Herzberg. New York: American Book, 1963, p. 364.

3. M. Twain, The Adventures of Huck Finn. Indianapolis: Bobbs-Merrill, 1967, p. 12.

4. N. Russe, "His Name Was Dean." Scope Music, Inc. BMI Forest Records, New York, 1955.

5. "James Dean, The Greatest of All," cited in D. Dalton, James Dean, The Mutant King. San Francisco: Straight Arrow Books, 1974, p. 316.

6. "The Ballad of James Dean," cited in D. Dalton, James Dean, The Mutant King. San Francisco: Straight Arrow Books, 1974, p. 316.

7. e. e. cummings, "Buffalo Bill," in Tulips and Chimneys. New York: Liveright, 1953, p. 85.

8. J. B. De La Faille, Vincent Van Gogh. New York: French and European Publications, 1939, p. 27.

9. E. Jong, "Two Entries from a Writer's Notebook," in The Other Pen. New York: P.E.N. American Center, 1975, p. 35.

10. D. McLean, "Starry Starry Night," American Pie. Capitol Records, New York, 1971.

11. R. Wilbur, "To An American Poet Just Dead," in Marvelous Light: Poets and Poetry, ed. H. Plotz. New York: Crowell, 1970, p. 115.

12. R. Anderson, I Never Sang for My Father. New York: New American Library, 1970, p. 113.

13. E. Hemingway, A Farewell to Arms. New York: Scribners, 1957, p. 116.

14. R. Herrick, "To the Virgins, To Make Much of Time," in Sound and Sense, ed. L. Perrine. New York: Harcourt, Brace, 1963, p. 76.

15. R. Herrick, "Corinna's Going A-Maying," in Sound and Sense, ed. L. Perrine. New York: Harcourt, Brace, 1963, pp. 274–276.

16. A. Marvell, "To His Coy Mistress," in *Sound and Sense*, ed. L. Perrine. New York: Harcourt, Brace, 1963, pp. 64–65.

17. E. Bronte, *Wuthering Heights*. New York: New American Library, 1959, pp. 30, 31, 343, 346, 352.

18. W. Faulkner, "A Rose for Miss Emily," in *The Portable Faulkner*, ed. M. Cowley. New York: Viking, 1929, pp. 433–444.

19. E. Dickinson, *Poems by Emily Dickinson*, ed. Bianchi and Hampson. Boston: Little Brown, 1914.

20. J. Donne, "A Valediction: Forbidding Mourning," in *The Complete English Poems*, ed. A. Smith. New York: St. Martins Press, 1971, p. 84.

21. S. Whitman, *Letters*. Cambridge, Mass.: Riverside Press, 1907, p. 252.

22. E. Hemingway, *For Whom the Bell Tolls*. New York: Scribners, 1940, p. 463.

23. D. Thomas, "And Death Shall Have No Dominion," in *A Reader's Guide*. New York: Noonday, 1962, p. 21.

24. R. Lichenstein, *Drowning Girl*. Museum of Modern Art, New York, 1960.

25. J. Taylor, "Fire and Rain," *Sweet Baby James*. Capitol Records, New York, 1970.

26. K. A. Porter, *Pale Horse, Pale Rider*. New York: New American Library, 1932.

27. J. Agee, *A Death in the Family*. New York: Avon, 1938, pp. 186–190.

28. J. Bowlby, "Processes of Mourning," *Int. J. Psychoanal*, 1961, 42, 317–340.

29. L. Caine, *Widow*. New York: Morrow, 1974, pp. 101–102.

30. *All The Way Home*, Paramount Pictures, California, 1940.

31. G. Santayana, "To W.P. II," in *Poems*. New York: Charles Scribners, 1901, pp. 60–61.

32. H. C. Andersen, "The Steadfast Tin Soldier," in *Andersen's Fairy Tales*. New York: Grosset & Dunlap, 1945, pp. 269–275.

33. H. C. Andersen, "The Little Match Girl," in *Andersen's Fairy Tales*. New York: Grosset & Dunlap, 1945, pp. 276–279.

34. F. Zefferelli, *Jesus of Nazareth*. Script by A. Burgess. London: Collins & World, 1977.

35. F. O'Connor, "The Lame Shall Enter First," in *Everything That Rises Must Converge*. New York: Farrar, Straus and Giroux, 1965, pp. 131–165.

36. W. Shakespeare, *The Tragedy of Antony and Cleopatra*, in *Shakespeare, The Complete Works*. New York: Harcourt, Brace, 1948, p. 1263.

37. W. Shakespeare, *The Tragedy of Romeo and Juliet,* in *Shakespeare, The Complete Works.* New York: Harcourt, Brace, 1948, p. 505.

38. S. Plath, "Daddy," in *Ariel.* New York: Harper & Row, 1961, p. 49.

39. J. M. Gerber, "The Cost Depends on What You Reckon It In," in *Stop Here, My Friend.* Boston: Houghton Mifflin, 1965, pp. 15–31.

40. M. Lazarus, *Momma, Boston Globe,* May 21, September 3, December 2, 1977.

41. H. McCracken, *George Catlin and the Old Frontier.* New York: Dial, 1969, p. 35. Painting on exhibit in Public Library, New York.

42. J. Herman, "Hymn to Hymie," *Milk and Honey,* RCA Victor, New York, 1961.

43. R. Anderson, "Notes of a Survivor," in *The Patient, Death, and the Family.* New York: Charles Scribners, 1974, p. 82.

44. O. Hammerstein and R. Rogers, "You'll Never Walk Alone," *Carousel,* MCA Record Co., Universal City, Calif., 1940.

45. W. Shakespeare, *The Tragedy of Hamlet, Prince of Denmark,* in *Shakespeare, The Complete Works.* New York: Harcourt, Brace, 1948, pp. 885–934.

46. C. Dickens, *A Christmas Carol.* Philadelphia: Lippincott, 1915.

47. I. B. Singer, "The Dead Fiddler," in *The Seance and Other Stories.* New York: Farrar, Straus and Giroux, 1968, pp. 36–55.

48. J. Thurber, "The Night the Ghost Got In," in *My Life and Hard Times.* New York: Harper & Row, 1933, pp. 52–66.

49. I. B. Singer, "Two Corpses Go Dancing," in *The Seance and Other Stories.* New York: Farrar, Straus and Giroux, 1968, pp. 187–201.

50. *Star Wars,* Twentieth Century Fox Films, New York, 1977.

51. A. Pushkin, *The Queen of Spades,* in *Great Russian Short Stories,* New York: Dell, 1958, pp. 19–47.

52. A. E. Housman, "Is My Team Ploughing," in *Sound and Sense,* ed. L. Perrine. New York: Harcourt, Brace 1963, pp. 22–23.

53. T. Wilder, *Our Town,* in *Three Plays.* New York: Bantam, 1938, pp. 52–62.

54. *The New Testament,* King James Edition. Glasgow: Collins, 1943.

55. L. Andreyev, "Lazarus," in *Return to Life: Two Imaginings of the Lazarus Theme.* New York: Arno, 1977, pp. 9–31.

56. E. O'Neill, *Lazarus Laughed,* in *The Plays of Eugene O'Neill.* New York: Random House, 1919, pp. 273–371.

57. R. Browning, "Mr. Sludge, 'The Medium,' " in *The Poems and Plays of Robert Browning.* New York: Random House, 1934, pp. 327–347.

58. *The Holy Scriptures*, Masoretic Text. New York: Jewish Publication Society of America, 1917.

59. *Fiddler on the Roof*, RCA, New York, 1976.

60. I. B. Singer, "The Seance," in *The Seance and Other Stories*. New York: Farrar, Straus and Giroux, 1968, pp. 7–14.

61. J. R. Lowell, *The Poetical Works of James Russell Lowell*, Vol. II. Boston: Houghton Mifflin, 1925, pp. 297–298.

62. L. Tolstoy, *The Death of Ivan Ilych and Other Stories*. New York: New American Library, 1960, p. 98.

63. E. L. Masters, *Spoon River Anthology*. New York: Collier Books, 1962.

64. E. Wasserman, *Gravestone Designs*. New York: Dover, 1972, p. 3.

65. A. Kull, *New England Cemeteries*. Brattleboro, Vt.: Stephen Greene Press, 1975, pp. 124–126.

66. D. Linnett, "Gifts," *Ms. Magazine*, March, 1978, pp. 67–71.

67. M. Kumin, "How It Is," *The New Yorker*, March 3, 1975.

68. V. Woolf, *The Waves*, in *Jacob's Room* and *The Waves*. New York: Harcourt, Brace, 1959, p. 367.

69. W. B. Yeats, "A Deep Sworn Vow," in *Selected Poems and Two Plays of William Butler Yeats*, ed. M. L. Rosenthal. New York: Macmillan, 1962, p. 43.

70. C. Zolotow, *My Grandson Lew*. New York: Harper & Row, 1974, pp. 24–32.

71. A. Sexton, "For Johnny Pole on the Forgotten Beach," in *To Bedlam and Part Way Back*. Boston: Houghton Mifflin, 1960, p. 32.

72. J. Romains, *The Death of a Nobody*. New York: New American Library, 1961, pp. 109–114.

73. S. Foster, "*Old Black Joe*."

74. *Bye Bye Braverman*, MGM Films, California, 1970.

75. W. B. Yeats, *The Dreaming of the Bones*, in *The Collected Plays of William Butler Yeats*. London: Macmillan, 1934, p. 433.

76. C. M. Parkes, "The First Year of Bereavement: A Longitudinal Study of the Reaction of London Widows to the Death of Their Husbands," *Psychiatry*, 1970, 33, 444–467.

# 9

# Death through the Retroscopic Lens

*Robert Kastenbaum*

*This is the place where the answers to the big questions would be given—if we had answers! What we actually have is just a way of thinking about the questions, as well as a selective review of the various types of methods and data that have been put forward over the years as possible support for a survival hypothesis.*

The condition "between life and death" is as exotic or as commonplace as we care to make it. Flora and fauna alive today draw nourishment from soil enriched by the organic remains of their ancestors. Each wave of living creatures is intimately related to those who went before and those who are yet to come. The physical death of the individual represents just one more transaction in the continuing business of the biosphere. From the microbiological perspective there is a perpetual shuttle running back and forth between the living and the nonliving—so indeed, we are warned that "misappreciation" of human burial places could upset the balance of nature (Nicoli, 1978). Microecology suggests that hardly anything is as commonplace and predictable as the multifarious transactions between "life" and "death."

The condition of "betweenness" is encountered at the distinctively human level as well:

- The individual poised at the brink of attempting suicide
- The person about to risk his or her life for life-affirming reasons (for example, to dash into a burning building to rescue a child)

•The soldier, the murderer, the hunter, the insect exterminator, anybody who is about to take the life of another living creature
•The person whose mental state is edging forward from haziness and lethargy to sensitivity and alertness—or who, by contrast, is slipping into coma and nonresponsiveness
•The individual who doctors his or her mind through drugs or alcohol to produce an experiential state of reduced consciousness

These are some of the examples that are familiar enough to us. The situations can be divided in general into those in which the physical survival of the person is at stake and those in which the deadening or enlivening of conscious experience is at stake.

If, then, we step back to appreciate the broad domain of human experience and action within the even broader domain of all nature, it is not necessary to regard the between-life-and-death condition as rare and exotic. It may be as commonplace as closing our eyes in the evening and opening them in the morning.

## Some Big Questions and Some Nearly as Big

We move closer now to the focus of this book. It seems to be that three big questions underlie much of what has been presented. "Is there survival of death?" seems to be the most basic question. This is a question that can and should be formulated more precisely. Who or what survives and the problem of exactly what is meant by survival need to be addressed carefully if we are to get anywhere with the inquiry. For the moment, however, let us simply acknowledge the question in its general form.

"Do we know enough to know whether or not our answer is accurate?" This is the second big question, which takes the first question as its point of reference. This is not idle word play. Imagine one person who is utterly convinced that there is survival of death. Now imagine another person who is just as convinced that there is no survival. The ordinary mind (one neither illuminated nor tormented by advanced skills in logical analysis) might conclude that the truth has been spoken. But by whom? Either the believer or the nonbeliever might possess the truth. Determining which belief is true is quite another matter. Such a determination might be easy, difficult, or impossible. The likelihood of being able to make this determination varies with one's philosophy of science or knowledge. It seems to me that legions of contemporary philosophers and sociobehavioral scientists have ignored the first question because they see no appropriate methodology for coping with the second question. We might, therefore, examine the material presented in this book to reevaluate this orientation. Are we now in any kind of position to improve our determination of the survival question? Do we have any data that really make a difference, or are we as far away from a solid answer as ever?

The third question has been the most shy in revealing itself. You will notice that the first two questions can be phrased in cognitive and objective or quasi-objective terms: "Is there survival?" "Can the survival question be answered?" (Or: "Is there a way of checking on the validity of our answer?") But the next question lays bare our hopes, fears, desires, ambitions, our fundamental sense of life's purpose: "*How should I live*, knowing that there is/is not survival of death?"

I doubt that intellectual curiosity has been the only force behind the first two questions. Isn't it instead the fact that the survival question has immense implications for the conduct of life? This is certainly a potent consideration for people who have been influenced since early childhood by religious views that link morality with whether one goes to heaven or hell. The connection may not be as direct and automatic for many people today as it was in past generations. Even the most atheistic of behavior modifiers, however, could fashion a parallel system. Reinforcements could be associated either with immediate, intermediate, or remote (afterlife) time frameworks. Still another way of putting it: Should we live for today? For the day after tomorrow? Or for eternity?

There are many interesting questions to consider that are of slightly less magnitude than the foregoing. Perhaps the most relevant of these second-magnitude questions is the following: "What are we to make of the data presented as evidence for or against survival if we put the survival question itself aside?" The purported phenomena, in other words, could be considered in themselves, apart from their supposed relationship to survival of death. "What are the effects of survival beliefs and communications on personality? On response to illness? On behavior in crisis situations?" These are examples of the questions that could be examined in this realm. Related questions include: "How are we to account for the cresting and fading of the various tides of experience that are alleged to bear on survival?" and "How are views concerning survival manipulated in our society—and for what motives?" One might detach all this material from its fundamental source—the question of survival— and concentrate on the nature, development, and influence of these experiences and ideas within the ordinary sphere of science and society. This is a fascinating and potentially useful line of inquiry in its own right—but it also strikes me as a neat evasion for the person who is not willing to touch the core of the problem.

This secondary line of inquiry might be supported as simply the most appropriate use of the scientific method: Let's study what can actually be studied instead of wasting effort (and appearing foolish) by jousting with windmills. But one might also liken this approach to the sexual teaser. Pleasure is derived from flirting with consequential possibilities. When glance comes to touch, however, the teaser departs or turns to stone. Has the time arrived when all systematic thinkers and researchers need to content themselves only with circumstantial and secondary approaches to the survival question? I am not ready to surrender the possibility that the survival question might prove amenable to a reasonably secure answer. Studies of the psychosocial context of the survival question and the phenomena and arguments that bedeck it can be important in helping us to achieve perspective, but need not substitute entirely for examination of the really big questions—or, at least, there is my bias exposed to plain view.

## The Survival Question: Evidence, Theories, Methods

The brief examination of the survival question that can be offered here is intended to sort out and concentrate observations that appear in many sources, including earlier sections of this book. Some of my own observations and opinions are represented, and these will generally be recognized by the context. So condensed a treatment of so challenging a subject cannot hope to offer more than a convenient takeoff place for those who are motivated to examine the problem more thoroughly. We are dealing here chiefly with the first two of the "big questions": Is there survival? How, if at all, might we go about determining and validating the "true" answer to this question? We will consider now some of the types of fact or purported fact that have been offered in evidence of survival hypotheses.

*Belief as Proof of Validity*

Belief in survival has been commonplace. The very fact that so many people throughout so much of human history have expressed belief in survival is sometimes presented as evidence. After all, how could so many people be mistaken?

The true-by-popularity type of evidence is no more persuasive here than in other domains. Other beliefs have been held by large numbers of people only to be demonstrated as incorrect (and sometimes even *after* being demonstrated as incorrect). The prevalence of belief in survival may provide evidence for certain motivational orientations. However, it is difficult to establish a clear link between belief and the objective status of survival. There are certainly alternative explanations for the prevalence of belief: Perhaps most people need to believe. Perhaps there are circumstances fairly common in human experience that have kindled such beliefs (and, as these circumstances alter, so may the beliefs). The fine-grained observer, whether of the historical or contemporary scene, will also note that the believers have not had the field entirely to themselves. There have been skeptics and "ambivalators" along with the believers through the years. Some people have experienced a crisis of doubt and faith, torn between the desire to believe and their own critical faculties. Furthermore, there has been such variety in the nature of the beliefs that it is difficult to add them all together, patch over their sometimes appreciable differences, and act as though they all signify the existence of essentially the same phenomenon.

There is an elitist variant of this type of evidence. Instead of counting up the number of people who hold or have held belief in survival, one might instead cite the more celebrated advocates. This list of elites could be assembled from philosophers, scientists, or any other type of person with call upon our respect. Yet a competitive list could be assembled from doubters and disbelievers. Intelligent, eminent, and charismatic individuals can be found on both sides of the fence, not to mention a goodly number who have taken up abode right on the fence.

There is still another variant to consider. *"I* believe in survival—therefore, it must be true!" How common this sentiment has been in other times and places I cannot say. It happens to be the most frequently expressed position that has come to my attention among people who hold for survival today in our supposedly educated, rational, and scientific climate. There have been philosophers and theologians who have gone to the trouble of developing theoretical frameworks that argue for the validity of such an egocentric or subjective position. Most who actually hold this view, however, are not party to either the rationales that they might draw on to strengthen their position or to the logical and scientific objections that others might array against them. To indulge in one of the great "buzz words" of the 1960s–1970s, it is usually a "gut level" orientation. If it could be demonstrated that there is a compelling link between strong personal conviction and objective reality, then the voice of the gut might indeed be taken as serious evidence. Such evidence—and even the felt need to produce such evidence—appears to be lacking, however. Parsimoniously, then, it appears more appropriate to leave the "I believe—therefore, it must be true!" position to those who are mostly interested in the personal and cultural dynamics of belief, rather than those who are searching for definitive evidence for or against the survival hypothesis.

The attempt to prove the reality of survival by citing either the number or the eminence of people who share this belief is probably the weakest type of evidence placed before us, and the same may be said of the unembellished personal belief orientation. I am among those who reject this class of purported evidence. But we should bear in mind precisely what is being rejected. The criticisms summarized above do not necessarily mean that the beliefs in survival are themselves mistaken. What they do mean is that the popularity and intensity of such beliefs cannot be taken as evidence for their validity. (This is the difference between "big questions" 1 and 2 again emphasized.)

*Encounters with the Dead*

We come now to a very broad class of possible evidence: *contact between the living and the dead*. A person believes that he or she has actually been in contact with somebody "on the other side." This type of evidence is different from what has already been touched on: there are perceptions, events or interactions to evaluate, as distinguished from attitudes and beliefs alone.

Reports of alleged contact between the living and the dead occur frequently in the anthropological literature and in many other sources. We will focus tightly on some of the efforts that have been made within the past hundred years to study and evaluate such experiences. This restriction omits much fascinating and instructive material. Nevertheless, it is only within the past hundred years that there have been systematic approaches—if few—that can be called at least protoscientific. Barbara Ross (chapter 3) has placed the development of "psychic research" in the last quarter of the nineteenth century within its more general intellectual context. We will pursue more specifically some of the major findings about and interpretations of the survival question.

*Ghosts, apparitions, phantasms.* These terms all point to one of the best-known and most obvious types of phenomena that have either given rise to or reinforced belief in survival. If I see a dead person or his "spirit," do I not have evidence that something or someone survives bodily death? The founders of the Society for Psychical Research (SPR) asked searching questions about the validity and nature of phenomena that today are known by terms such as "paranormal," "psychic," and "extrasensory perception." They were well aware of contemporary developments in the new depth psychology and often found that the material they collected could be interpreted in terms of suggestibility and other types of personality dynamics that do not require acceptance of either the survival hypothesis or paranormal abilities. It is clear, however, that the survival hypothesis was a core concern for these early investigators. They judged that existing information was not adequate to help them come to firm conclusions, nor were existing methodologies of much value. It was natural that in their pursuit of the survival hypothesis they would also come across many other phenomena that would have to be carefully sorted out, classified, and evaluated. The nucleus of SPR investigators was comprised of well-educated people with disciplined minds who were attempting to apply logic and scientific method to a field heretofore ruled by anecdotes and speculations. Although they lacked the accumulated knowledge and more advanced research techniques that later psychological scientists would acquire, they were "nobody's fools." Indeed, their work still provides admirable examples of how one might proceed into challenging and essentially unknown territory.

At first they cast a wide net and hauled in an assorted catch of reported experiences from people in all walks of life. These included, but were not limited to, possible encounters with ghosts and other apparitions. Many seemingly normal people recalled experiences of this general type. Some of the best-documented and most plausible reports were published in a two-volume work, *Phantasms of the Living* (Gurney, Podmore, and Myers, 1886). It is important to understand the attitude the authors took toward this material. Gurney in particular attempted to establish general criteria for examining alleged observations of apparitions of the dead. Let us remember that he was writing at a time when the concepts and techniques that today are invoked for the statistical analysis of data were in relatively early stages of development. His intentions were clear enough, however. Gurney emphasized that we cannot rely on quite the same principles when examining visions or phantasms associated with people who are still alive and those allegedly associated with the dead. SPR had investigated many incidents in which a person believed he or she had seen—and sometimes heard—another individual who was actually at that time alive but in another locale. These incidents were often associated with critical and life-threatening events, usually with some type of powerful emotion. Some form of "mental telepathy" was considered to be a potential explanation for these phenomena. Telepathy was held to be a relatively more conservative explanation as compared with the alternative view that a "double" of the living person had in reality been created and dispatched to the experiencer.

Gurney pointed out that we have reasonable expectations and guidelines for the behavior of living people, especially for particular individuals whose ways we know. It was at least theoretically possible to establish a probability baseline against which particular observations could be compared. Any given observation of a living person's "apparition" might then be checked against laws of probability or "coincidence" (the latter was the term Gurney actually used). The scientifically inclined investigator could attempt to establish standards of expectation or coincidence. These standards would have to be exceeded by a particular observation before it would be taken as evidence that something really exceptional had taken place.

It is quite different with the dead. If there are any behaviors, emanations, or whatever in this realm, we have no independent basis for knowing their rules and probabilities. "In alleged cases of apparitions of the dead, the point which we have held to distinguish certain apparitions of *living* persons from purely subjective hallucinations is necessarily lacking. That point is *coincidence* between the apparition and some critical or exceptional condition of the person who seems to appear; but with regard to the dead, we have no independent knowledge of their condition, and therefore never have the opportunity of observing any such coincidences" (Gurney, 1888, p. 403).

He recognized that the apparent manifestation of a dead person is best assumed to be a subjective phenomenon on the part of the percipient, a kind of hallucination, unless there is excellent reason to believe otherwise. Gurney proposed three conditions that could distinguish hallucination from an authentic manifestation: (1) More than one person has the experience or perception independently of another; (2) The phantasm conveys information unknown and not possibly knowable to the percipient at the time but later confirmed; or (3) The phantom is a detailed manifestation of a person previously unknown to the percipient and yet it can be shown to be clearly a definitive identification. These become standard criteria for serious investigators.

The cases presented and discussed in *Phantasms of the Living* offered a rich basis for further speculation but were subject to many limitations from an evidential standpoint. This was well appreciated by the SPR investigators, who knew that their work had just begun. A few years later they were able to report on a "census of hallucinations" (the major publication here: Sidgwick, 1894). This was an international effort that resulted in the collection of approximately 17,000 interview protocols. The central question was: "Have you ever, when believing yourself to be completely awake, had a vivid impression of seeing or being touched by a living being or inanimate object, or of hearing a voice; which impression, so far as you could discover, was not due to any external physical cause?" Approximately one respondent in ten had an experience to report, occasionally multiple experiences. These were classified into a variety of categories, not all of which concern us here. Many reports were rejected for further consideration as being products of dreams or delirium as contrasted with lucid waking experience. The mass of reports quickly melted down as the SPR committee examined them. Eventually they had eighty cases that involved well-described apparitions of people who had died twelve hours or less before the manifestation occurred. These seemed to be the most promising cases in light of Gurney's fourth criterion and his associated speculations about the type of evidence that might hold the most promise of being solid. The SPR investigators tightened their requirements even further: Were there any cases in which it could be demonstrated that the percipient had described the experience to one or more people before learning of the death of the person who had become manifest to him? A smaller set of thirty-two cases remained when this criterion was applied. One could choose to be either encouraged or discouraged by this yield. About 17,000 people from many walks of life were interviewed, and only thirty-two "good" cases remained (based on the criteria applied by the investigators)—but yet, there, indeed, were thirty-two good cases!

The SPR investigators then did something with these instances that was rather exceptional for its day. They attempted to test the null hypothesis that the thirty-two deceased people might have been seen "by chance" within twenty-four hours of their death by using available statistical tables on the odds of an individual dying on a particular day. They concluded that the obtained frequency was approximately 440 times greater than what would have been expected on the basis of chance. It is not difficult to second-guess and criticize the particular statistical test performed and the assumptions it made. However, the analytic effort itself demonstrates the serious intent of the SPR at this point in its history to use the most advanced available techniques to evaluate evidence on so challenging a topic as alleged apparitions of the dead.

In the meantime, the SPR continued to collect and investigate cases that came to its attention from a variety of sources. Many reports were too incomplete or dubious for the investigators to take seriously. Even the best cases could not be said to provide definitive proof that a living person had actually experienced contact with a deceased person or his "spirit," "ghost," or what-have-you. Years of subsequent investigation did not seem to appreciably alter the picture summarized by Eleanor Balfour Sidgwick (1885). But some cases appeared to stand up well against the criterion of multiple percipients. When several people had reported the same phenomenon, it was difficult to explain the observations away as individual hallucinations (not impossible, just difficult). This left open the possibility of group hallucinations, of course, as well as other explanations. Nevertheless, these cases did comprise a core of reports that met fairly rigorous standards of evidence and were not easy prey to the usual objections. The typical case almost seemed to fit the traditional specifications for a "haunting." Almost.

Even the most promising hauntings had to be disappointing to those who might have been expecting the SPR investigations to prove the reality behind the ghost stories. Sightings there were, but the stories were not forthcoming. The phantasms did not seem to say or do much of anything. All the "ghosts" put together from the best cases failed to provide instances that would have met Gurney's criteria. The apparitions did not have strange and illuminating things to say—usually they said not a word, nor did they seem embarked on some clear purpose. In this regard the "ghosts" who were properly registered and filed by the SPR parted company with their more flamboyant counterparts in fiction and folklore. They were simply—how one hesitates to use the term—dull!

Frederic W. H. Myers recognized the situation clearly as he was preparing his majestic two-volume work, *Human Personality and Its Survival of Bodily Death* (completed by his friends and published posthumously in 1903). Apparitions and ghosts were among only a few of the topics Myers systematically reviewed, organized, and discussed. He could see that the "research ghosts" were but pale and relatively uninteresting figures in comparison with the more colorful manifestations that glower in Shakespeare or glow around campfire conversations. What should be made of such a finding? Myers confirms that "there is strong evidence for the recurrence of the same hallucinatory figures in the same localities, but weak evidence to indicate any purpose in most of these figures, or any connection with bygone individuals, or with such tragedies as are popularly supposed to start a ghost on its career." In some of these cases of the frequent, meaningless recurrence of a figure in a given spot, we are driven to wonder whether it can be some deceased person's past frequentation of that spot, rather than any fresh action of his after death, that has generated an "after-image" (1903, vol. 2, p. 4).

The specific peculiarities of the reported manifestations led Myers to develop the after-image theory that is touched upon in the preceding passage. It also led him to offer an interesting argument for phenomena whose reality was more than subjective, no matter how one might choose to explain them:

> The very fact that such bizarre problems should present themselves at every turn does in a certain sense tend to show that these apparitions are not purely subjective things—do not originate merely in the percipient's imagination. *For they are not like what any man would have imagined.* What man's mind does tend to fancy on such topics may be seen in the endless crop of fictitious ghost stories, which furnish, indeed, a curious proof of the persistence of preconceived notions. For they go on being framed according to canons of their own, and deal with a set of imaginary phenomena quite different from those which actually occur. The actual phenomena, I may add, could scarcely be made romantic. . . . And thus, absurdly enough, we sometimes hear men ridicule the phenomena which actually do happen, simply because those phenomena do not suit their preconceived notions of what ghostly phenomena ought to be;—not perceiving that this very divergence, this very unexpectedness, is in itself no slight indication of an origin *outside* the minds which obviously were so far from anticipating anything of the kind. (Myers, vol. 2, p. 5) [emphasis added]

William James was one of the first to appreciate Myers's ability to cleave a path between culturally perpetuated notions of ghosts and certain phenomena that were reported with a measure of empirical regularity and consistency, yet which seemed to be outside the traditional sphere of expectations. James noted that

In comparison with Myers's way of attacking the problem of immortality . . . the official way is certainly so far from the mark as to be almost preposterous. It assumes that when our ordinary consciousness goes out, the only alternative surviving kind of consciousness that could be possible is abstract mentality, living on spiritual truth, and communicating ideal wisdom—in short, the whole classic platonizing Sunday-school conception. Failing to get that sort of thing when it listens to reports about mediums, it denies that there can be anything. Myers approaches the subject with no such *a priori* requirement. If he finds any positive indication of "spirits," he records it, whatever it may be, and is willing to fit his conception to the facts, however grotesque the latter may appear, rather than to blot out the facts to suit his conception. (James, 1901/1961, pp. 223–224).

Myers's synthesis of available data around the turn of the century could not entirely please either the true believers or the determined skeptics. There did seem to be some data that a responsible person would not lightly discard, yet these data deviated from expectations and could lend themselves to a variety of explanations (in addition to Myers's own after-image theory). At about this time the focus of psychical research began to move in other directions, especially to phenomena associated with "mediums" (as noted in the passage quoted from James). It should be emphasized that this swing of attention did not mean that the existence of evidence for apparitions had been thoroughly settled for once and all. There are fads and fashion in research as well as in other social systems, as most of us know very well.

Although the spotlight roved elsewhere, interest in apparitions as possible data for survival after death did not completely disappear. There was a brief flirtation with "spirit photography," for example. As the term suggests the main items here were photographs that purported to show materialized spirits of the deceased or their "ectoplasmic" fragments right there in black and white. The verdict came in quickly: inconclusive at best, undoubtedly fraudulent in some if not most instances, overall, not serious evidence. "Haunted houses" have continued to be examined around the world, sometimes with fairly elaborate investigative techniques. One cannot say that firm evidence of more-than-subjective events has been added to what was known in Myers's time. The naïveté with which some people have accepted "spirit photography" and "hauntings" over the years has perhaps made these approaches so susceptible to doubt and parody that it is difficult for serious investigators to take them up. Gertrude Schmeidler (1966) has shown that behaviorally oriented methodology can be applied to the study and analysis of "hauntings." To "prove" that there really is or has been an encounter between the living and the dead, however, remains a challenge that so far appears to have overmatched existing methodologies.

At least two other types of apparition data should be mentioned. Many anecdotal reports over the years have suggested that people who are seriously ill or at the very point of death sometimes behave as though in contact with beings who are not visible to others. Karlis Osis conducted a systematic survey of such observations, calling on the reported experiences of physicians and nurses (Osis, 1961). More recently, he has offered an extensive follow-up study that also includes data from India (Osis and Haraldsson, 1977). The information collected by Osis and Haraldsson is easily accessible through their writings; each reader can work toward his or her own conclusions. They seem to have come up with a fair amount of internal consistency among reports collected from a variety of sources; furthermore, these reports (like those reviewed by Myers) often diverge from what one might have expected on the basis of religious and cultural traditions. These two aspects of their findings might be regarded as lending at least indirect support to the existence of phenomena that are more than subjective hallucinations. As usual, however, there are a variety of explanations to choose from (some are discussed by Osis and Haraldsson), and the hypothesis of survival after death is seldom the most parsimonious. The data presentation sections of the Osis and Haraldsson book have the mark of being faithful to the variety of material obtained (as distinguished from being regimented to defend a preselected position). The discussion and opinions sections provide the sort of challenges to which one has become accustomed after tuning into a multilogue that has been in progress for many years. The one point I feel obliged to bring out here is that even a more mountainous buildup of data of the type collected by Osis and Haraldsson seems unlikely to provide a critical test of the survival hypothesis. Gurney's logical criteria for distinguishing "hallucination" from a more-than-subjective apparition do not appear to be met in most instances. A person in a crisis situation may appear to be experiencing contact with another being (and may even be able to give some report of this contact), but it does not seem to be in the nature of things for other observers to have direct confirmation of the encounter.

For a particularly innovative approach to "ghosts," one might turn to the creators of "Philip." A subgroup of the Toronto Society for Psychical Research took up a theory proposed by Kenneth J. Batcheldor (1966) and decided to produce its own manifestations. In essence, this view holds that most if not all "ghosts" who appear to become manifest through the senses are in fact creations and projections of the human mind. The actual phenomenon can be physicalistic and in that sense "objective," but their source is to be found in the subjective or psychic realm. *Conjuring Up Philip* (Owen and Sparrow, 1976) traces the deliberate creation of a "ghost" by a group of people who knew right from the start that they were trying to cultivate a sort of mass or field psychic effect rather than enter into contact with a "real" ghost. The Philip experiment (and its several follow-ups) seems to have produced physical phenomena such as a "talking table," but no visual manifestations such as those reported for "real" ghosts (for example, as in the Sidgwick and Myers data) or ghosts from folklore or fiction. Not everyone will evaluate the evidence produced by the Philip group in the same way, but we have here at least a determined attempt to *experiment* with the production of "ghosts" based on a theoretical model. It remains to be seen whether or not the experimental (as distinguished from the merely descriptive or empirical) approach will be followed up vigorously or if it will soon fall by the wayside because of the labors and challenges involved.

*Theories* about apparent "ghosts" have continued to be offered over the years. Notable presentations and discussions include works by Tyrrell (1962) and Hart (1959). While some theories are relatively specific to apparitions, the general ideas tend to apply to many types of data that bear on the survival question. In particular, one is often asked to choose between a survival-oriented explanation and one that assumes some form of paranormal functioning on the part of the living. This latter type of explanation is sometimes known as "super-ESP." It has often been invoked as an alternative explanation in the realm of mediumistic activities (to be discussed below). The theories outlined by Myers, James, and others of their time still have not been thoroughly tested and evaluated. These early theories, and some of the more recent ones, involve interesting speculations about the basic dynamics and functioning of the human mind. In attempting to follow the survival hypothesis wherever it might lead, then, some thinkers have come up with ideas whose range of application is more extensive than even this mighty topic itself. Since I am not about to present and evaluate other people's theories about apparitions here, it would hardly be fair to present any of my own. A few things may be said in summary, however: (1) There is no shortage of theories related to the survival hypotheses; (2) These range from explanations that entirely reject any form of survival to those which would support the persistence of individual personality after death; while (3) Some of the most interesting theories center around processes and dynamics that are alternatives to usual conceptions of survival or total rejection of interaction between the living and the once-living.

A person might well turn away from the entire theory-spinning process on grounds that the data are not firm enough to warrant such exercises. Certainly, one could hardly say the data are *too* firm! I am not so sure that we would be justified in sweeping all the observations away because they are puzzling, incomplete, and lacking something in methodological purity. Rejection or continued interest may simply be a matter of temperament at this point. Perhaps a high tolerance for cognitive ambiguity is needed—or simply the tendency to be fascinated by such a challenge to logic, observation, and judgment. At the least, it seems to me that attention to the alleged phenomena and to the tortuous attempts at explanation reveals facets of psychology that are seldom illuminated by more routine pursuits.

It remains to be said that at least one type of data brought to the surface in the ghost-tracking operations is important in the more established area of present-day thanatology. Reference is made to Gurney's analysis and discussion of the time distribution of manifestations (in *Phantasms of the Living*). Today there is a much greater accumulation of information about the experiences and behaviors of people who have been recently bereaved (for example, Kastenbaum,

1977; Parkes, 1972). It is common for people to have a pronounced sense of the "presence" of the deceased loved one in the period immediately after death. This can take the form of both waking and dream experiences and appear in either vague or precise forms. The empirical finding that there is more sense of contact with the dead soon after death appears to hold, but there are explanations of a psychodynamic type that appear more satisfactory and parsimonious than those which would support a more-than-subjective basis. As we have already said in other contexts, the fact that there are more parsimonious or less "far out" explanations does not invalidate the survival hypothesis; it just deprives us of the opportunity to demonstrate that the survival hypothesis is the one best equipped to account for the phenomena.

*Contact with the dead through mediums.* Who is capable of communicating with the dead? One tradition emphasizes the possibility that anybody might have such encounters. The early work of the SPR and such recent studies as those of Osis and Haroldsson exemplify this approach. It is also consistent with the view that paranormal abilities in general are distributed normally through the population, in more or less the same fashion as we assume a number of other abilities are distributed.

However, another tradition emphasizes the exceptional abilities of a few people. This tradition has its ancient heroes—seers, wizards, prophets, and the like—as well as its contemporary luminaries. Anton Mesmer could be described as the very model of such a person even though he is not classified among the mediums. Mesmer, who believed he was bending "animal magnetism" to healing purposes, was a prototype for the hypnotist and the psychoanalyst who (in the eye of the beholder) manifests mysterious and remarkable powers, as well as for the stage magician who mimes and parodies occult power. Mesmer appeared to be an individual in whom unusual powers were concentrated. "Fortune tellers" and others have claimed special psychic powers. Often they have attempted to bolster their cause with gimmickry, environmental aids, confederates, and self-dramatization. The image of the quasi-medical, authoritarian healer (or menace) and that of the coldly scheming fraud have to be laid out in order to be laid aside. Individual malpractitioners have been discredited regularly and many of their techniques exposed. The prevalence of fraud and trickery has created a lingering sense that one had best stay away completely from any purported evidence for the survival hypothesis that might be associated with so-called mediums.

The oft-burned believer and the resolute skeptic understandably may view the literature on mediumship with dismay. However, there are enough exceptions to the usual run of fraud and trickery to challenge the open-minded observer. Some of the apparently most adept "mediums" were people whose lives could not have been more "respectable," who profited not at all from their special gifts, and who made themselves available to critical scrutiny over prolonged periods of time. This is not to claim that either separately or cumulatively they have provided incontrovertible evidence for some type of survival hypothesis. It is just hard to see how the observations made about such mediums as Mrs. Piper and Mrs. Leonard could be dismissed without serious consideration. The most challenging and fully reported cases do at least give one pause.

Fortunately, there is an accessible literature on mediumship in general and its relationship to possible contacts with "discarnate spirits." Reliable starting points for inquiry include contributions by Douglas (1976), Salter (1961), and Gauld (1977). There are also full-length biographies and in-depth studies on some of the more celebrated mediums. Two autobiographies by the late American medium Eileen Garrett (1939; 1968) may be of special interest both for their recentness and for her advocacy of scientific method (leading directly to the establishment of the Parapsychology Foundation in New York City). Our discussion here is a very brief one, not because the topic is lacking in rich material, but because other sources may be easily consulted.

So-called mediums most often have communicated their messages through their own voices in "trance states" or in "automatic writing." The provocative episodes have been those in which information has been conveyed that apparently could have been known only to a deceased person, not to the medium. Even more provocative have been those episodes in which the "sitters" also were not aware of the information and had to resort to external validation checks to confirm the details. As we might expect, critics have been on the lookout for any possibility that the medium could have used subtle cues from the sitters in developing the information. In the most thoroughly investigated mediumships, this possibility was carefully evaluated, and control measures taken (although seldom if ever can one be certain beyond the shadow of a doubt that some extremely subtle type of interpersonal communication has not occurred). There have also been numerous experiments and tricks played on mediums by their investigators. Mrs. Piper, a Bostonian who was studied on both sides of the Atlantic, seems to have survived a series of such challenges put to her by several generations of critically attuned investigators.

When the "data" themselves appear hard to discredit, there has remained the question of explanation. The super-ESP hypothesis continues to be a strong rival to the survival hypothesis. Wouldn't it be less mind-boggling to accept the possibility that an individual is enormously gifted with telepathic or clairvoyant powers than to accept the alternative of actual communication with the dead? Some efforts have been proposed, and occasionally made in practice, to reject the SESP hypothesis. One strategy has been to keep the person who really has a question to ask or a piece of information to check out away from the medium. A "proxy sitter" may be interposed, thereby attenuating the possibility of telepathic (or other form of subtle) communication between the living. One might, in fact, introduce a whole concatenation of proxy individuals to widen the gap. And yet, should the medium still come forth with detailed information specific to a deceased person, the advocate of the SESP hypothesis need not necessarily retire gracefully. The SESP position is so vaguely defined, so without dimensions and limits, that it could conceivably be stretched to accommodate any data. There is a kind of standoff in effect, then. Given an apparent example of "good data" from a medium, should the material be explained in terms of this "black box" (super-ESP) or that one (actual communication with the dead)? So very little is known about either of these hypothetical phenomena that advocates of one position or the other might hold their ground indefinitely if they choose to do so and no new methodological or evidential breakthrough arrives on the scene to compel a change.

But is it possible that a "breakthrough" has actually been

achieved but not appreciated? Consider this possibility: After an individual dies, he somehow arranges for messages to be disseminated in a type of code. Furthermore, the messages are doled out piecemeal among several different mediums or receivers. The total message does not come through, does not make sense, until all the pieces are assembled from the various mediums. Let us make the conditions even more interesting. Some of the "receivers" do not know each other until their bits of message start coming in; further, some of them scarcely have an inkling ahead of time that they possess any special gift for receiving such communications. Let us add still another twist: Questions, riddles, and challenges can be put to the deceased through one or more of the mediums. The reply to these specific inquiries will also come through multiple person-channels. Furthermore, all the messages will bear marks of the deceased's individual personality, sense of humor, passions, and quirks, and not be merely arcane pieces of information.

What I have just described is the *cross-correspondence* vein of experience and research. Have such phenomena actually occurred? Is the evidence sufficient to support belief in personal survival after death? Every person would have to come to his or her own conclusion on these matters—and this discloses at once a major difficulty in evaluating both mediumship experiences in general and the exceptionally provocative cross-correspondences in particular. The mass of material is enormous; the task of properly decoding and checking it seems overwhelming. For an introduction to this topic, one might do well to begin with the chapter in Douglas's (1976) useful book and then adventure along to the classic little monograph by Saltmarsh (1938/1975). The first instance of cross-correspondences started with apparent postmortem communications from F. W. H. Myers, the distinguished scholar who played a significant role in the establishment and early activities of the SPR. Detail is of such critical importance in understanding and evaluating the possible validity of the cross-correspondences that we could not usefully summarize the material here. Perhaps it is enough to indicate that a potential method has been described that just might provide critical evidence for the survival hypothesis—furthermore, at least some careful and systematic investigators believe the method has actually been utilized. Is it merely an idle thought to imagine a computer-assisted evaluation of existing information on cross-correspondences, as well as a possible *prospective* study aimed toward communication with deceaseds-to-be? The extensive development of information-processing technology since the turn of the century might be applied to creative and effective use here.

*Reincarnation.* The survival hypothesis takes on quite a different aspect when we permit ourselves to consider reincarnation as a possibility. Some of our core assumptions about the nature of reality (and about what constitutes rational or acceptable thought) in the Western world make it difficult to take evidence favoring survival after death seriously. These assumptions include the view of time as essentially linear, directional, as well as the dependence of "mind" on "matter," and a fundamental cleavage between the individual person and the rest of the universe. Given assumptions of this type, it is difficult to be fully responsive to discrete bits of evidence that might otherwise seem to support survival. The *quest* for evidence itself and the stringent (if not entirely consistent) requirements we establish for satisfactory evidence also are part of our particular world view. The Eastern perspective on death has developed within a different context of assumptions. Reincarnation is an article of faith that is not generally seen as in need of laborious empirical or logical support. The idea of reincarnation is a "better fit" with Eastern conceptions of time, causality, and the nature of the universe than it is with the dominant ideas of the West. This divergent approach to the essential nature of the universe makes it difficult to examine the (to us) hypothetical process of reincarnation in an evenhanded manner. It would probably be most convenient to reject reincarnation instantly because the very concept seems out of place in the type of conceptual universe we believe we should believe we are inhabiting. And it might be almost as convenient to rebel against our own upbringing (often an exhilarating experience!) and simply replace it with its Eastern counterpart. Certainly, there are and always have been Westerners who have come to prefer the Eastern view, and one can make the case that there is something in the early childhood experiences of all people that lends intuitive support to this view (Kastenbaum & Aisenberg, 1972, chapter 2). If we are less interested in making things easy for ourselves, however, and more intent on following ideas and observa-

tions wherever they might lead, then the possibility of reincarnation raises complex questions related to the survival hypothesis.
The reader might first fortify himself by reviewing historical and
philosophical background material associated with reincarnation
(for example, Lee, 1974, for a recent and lucid treatise).

Anecdotal reports of purported reincarnations have been circulat-
ing since who knows when. One person has finally taken up the
challenge of tracking down "cases suggestive of reincarnation" and
subjecting them to reasonable investigation and analysis. Ian Stevenson, a psychiatrist on the University of Virginia faculty, has
developed a systematic technique for examining possible examples
of reincarnation. His work is reported in greatest detail in a book
focusing on twenty cases (Stevenson, 1974), but he has also discussed the subject in a number of articles (for example, Stevenson,
1977). A section of *The Journal of Nervous and Mental Disease* was
recently devoted to a presentation and commentary on his work (15,
3, September, 1977).

What Stevenson has to offer can be readily evaluated by each
reader, for his method and tentative findings are presented in ex-
plicit detail. One could hardly ask for a clearer, better organized
presentation of material that must be extracted from the complexities of "real life" situations. Apparently, he also has voluminous
unpublished material that is awaiting further investigation and
analysis.

The typical case "suggestive of reincarnation" (Stevenson's own
cautious phrase) involves a young child whose behavior and conversation imply a specific previous existence. Many of his published cases are from Eastern or relatively "undeveloped" nations,
but it is understood that he has comparable cases on file from the
United States and other technologically oriented societies. The
families of such children are not invariably persuaded by these
behaviors, at least at first. Striking details and "coincidences" eventually lead them to take the phenomena more seriously. In his own
active investigations, Stevenson checks and cross-checks information bearing on the purported reincarnations. As with apparitions
and mediums, some cases seem more evidential than others. Quite
unlike most of the apparition reports, the reincarnation phenomena
often seems to have motivational and purposive components (for

example, a very young child behaves as though he had once been murdered by having his throat slashed in a previous incarnation—and does, in fact, have a birthmark on his throat that could pass for a scar). In the more evidential cases, the alternative hypotheses of information obtained through usual channels by guesswork or even by telepathy/clairvoyance are not easy to sustain.

Stevenson offers interesting speculations on the possible significance of reincarnation experiences across a spectrum of developmental behavior and considers a number of alternative hypotheses to the basic "reborn" interpretation. He seems to be successful so far in keeping his own opinion private in an effort to avoid unduly influencing the reader.

It is doubtful if Stevenson's work will be accepted by many as strong evidence for the survival hypothesis until such data themselves survive a process of multiple cross-validations. Other investigators will have to be ready to devote the time, care, and energy necessary to explore "cases suggestive of reincarnation" by Stevenson's method and by other appropriate methods that can be devised. At the moment it is too early to determine whether or not there will be any takers for this challenge.

*Clinical death or near-death experiences.* Much of the material discussed in this book bears on the near-death experience. *If* we are satisfied with such terms as "clinical death," "near death," or "crisis experiences," then these reports retain considerable interest—but not as direct support for any form of survival. It would be easy enough to play with words in either direction: to *define* the state of the experiencing individual as either "dead" or "not dead" and make this definition bear the full weight of responsibility. Such an approach would award temporary honors to the most clever, authoritarian, or elusive slinger of verbal nets, but would not much advance our knowledge.

There are both advantages and limitations to these data as data (and please understand that my persistent focus on the evidential aspects of the phenomena is not intended to convey disinterest in their personal meanings and possible therapeutic implications). Perhaps the most obvious advantage is the fact that the "deceased" is available to report the experience and to respond to questions about it. This is much more satisfying then relying on inarticulate ghosts and "spirit controls" whose communication through "mediums" often leaves much to be desired. Related to this advantage is the fact that often there are multiple observers who were in position to view the events from the outside while the protagonist was undergoing the subjective experience. A mass of information, some of it quite objective and already in quantified form, can at times be collected to add supplementary dimensions (for example, vital signs, laboratory findings, detailed information on treatment procedures). The incidents sometimes have occurred over a fairly extended period of time, as constrasted with evanescent views of apparitions. Theoretically, one might also learn to recognize situations in which a "life after life" experience is most likely to arise. This could make it possible to improve both observations and helpful interventions.

Limitations include the gap that remains between objective observation and the subjective realm. Even if the person between life and death were carefully monitored with EEG and other measurements, this would not necessarily prove anything about the survival hypothesis. Such information would certainly be of interest—but it might be naïve to expect that subjective experience could be translated into objective assessment (or vice versa) any more reliably in this realm than in the much broader realm of psychophysical phenomena in general. We might *learn* useful facts and acquire promising *insights* from improved observation techniques, in other words, but it is a little much to expect these to yield definitive answers to the survival hypothesis. Moreover, in actual (as distinguished from idealized possible) instances, there is probably no such being as an "objective observer." The people on the scene have emotional responses and, frequently, pragmatic roles to carry out.

There is another problem, which entangles us in semantics to some extent. The people who return with experiences to share may have been "dead," if our choice of definitions in an ambiguous situation takes that direction. But—awkward to say!—the person does not seem to have been "as dead" as one whose physical deterioration had become more advanced. The body, although stressed, still exists as an entity. The reports do not come from those who have passed into rigor mortis or decomposition. The more physical evidence there is of death (in the usual sense of the term), the less likely the return and the report. "Life after life" experiences, then, if they do come from "once-dead" people, come from those who were not "as dead as one can be." This suggests that data from this one type of experience may not be sufficient to test a survival hypothesis even when it is available in its strongest form.

Other problems with these experiences as data have been touched on in this book. Let us single out one problem that appears to characterize *all* the sources of data for the survival hypothesis.

*If one, or a few, why not all?* Grant the possibility that what seem to be ghosts or apparitions are sometimes ghosts or apparitions. The sightings appear to be relatively uncommon when we consider the frequency of death itself. One could ask the usual question: How could there be any ghost, even one, any time, under any circumstance? Or one could ask a different question: If there are perhaps ghosts on occasion, why not more often? Why doesn't every deceased person yield a spirit that is somehow perceived by the survivors? A similar inquiry may be lodged of the "discarnate minds" that have occasionally seemed to communicate through "mediums" in reasonably convincing fashion. Why don't we hear from the dead all the time, or at least more commonly? Is the problem the short supply of authentic mediums? The inability or lack of fine tuning that keeps most of us from receiving messages? Can it be that only a few deceased people choose to communicate, or that only a few can? More radically, perhaps: Is it the case that a few humans survive death in some form, but that most do not? This concept is not entirely unknown (for example, Hocking's theory of "conditional immortality"). It would raise a problem for most people who are accustomed to thinking in terms of general laws or principles that govern the universe. What goes up must come down—but only sometimes! One and one make two, but sometimes three, and sometimes make nothing at all! Twentieth-century science (notably theoretical physics) has provided us with alternative conceptions of the universe that still do not seem at home with our intuitive or conditioned sense of "how things really are." Possibly, some people die and stay dead while others do not. Such a notion would take some getting used to. At the moment it stands as one more obstacle to accepting survival explanations of phenomena such as apparitions and mediumistic communications.

The problem is with us again perhaps even more exquisitely

when we look over Stevenson's shoulder to examine "cases suggestive of reincarnation." The most persuasive cases are the very ones that make me wonder: Why should reincarnation be so rare, if it happens at all? One might argue that it is not really that rare. We just are not very sensitive to reincarnation phenomena and miss many examples. And yet—the most evidential cases appear to be quite different from patterns of normal development. Millions of children seem to grow up without proclaiming or manifesting previous incarnations. To accept reincarnation as an *occasional* phenomenon may require as much intellectual struggle as the acceptance of reincarnation as a basic and universal phenomenon. Note that for this latter alternative one would need data that go beyond any that now seem to be available; by contrast, it would take absolute proof for only *one* of Stevenson's cases to establish reincarnation as an actual if occasional phenomenon.

Data such as those cited by Garfield (chapter 4) and noted on a less systematic basis by myself indicate that "life after life" cases also represent only a fraction of those who have been in the borderlands. Clinical explanations (for example, the provocative ideas offered by Noyes, chapter 6) would seem to have a stronger hold on our attention if there are differential responses to the near-death experience. If there is only one state of "deadness," why is it that some people seem to return with a particular story to tell, while others do not?

I am aware that the questions I have been raising in this section can be answered in a hasty and patchwork fashion. I urge more patience. It is not that I want to pose questions that leave the believer or advocate for survival speechless. I simply wish to have emphasized a point not previously brought out—namely, that we may have a choice ahead of either setting aside much data because they imply more than one kind of death or of readjusting our minds to taking this possibility seriously.

## A Concluding Thought or Two

"New Data or Same Old Story?" was the question I raised to myself as well as to my colleagues in psychology in organizing the symposium that generated this book. I felt the need to gain some perspective on what had been done in the past as well as what was going on today. This chapter has given me one more opportunity to employ that marvellous, if nonexistent, instrument, the retroscope. Had we really a retroscope at our disposal we would have a more adequate view of the ways in which minds—including some of the best ever to come along—have confronted the question of survival. Furthermore, we might set the retroscope on a sort of electronic time delay, and thereby see ourselves and our own efforts as they might be viewed from future perspective. Lacking this sophisticated instrumentation, I can only share my impression that there is more continuity between past and present efforts to comprehend the possibility of survival than we might have previously believed. We are not *so* different from past generations in this respect, but we do have methodologies available in the behavioral science and concepts in many areas of science that might be applied to the survival question had we the inclination to do so.

I do not think we have made as much use of the most promising materials from the past as we might have, nor have we fully addressed the logical and methodological questions of emerging phenomena. Even parapsychology, in some respects quite a sophisticated field today, has not been making what one could describe as a wholehearted effort to test the survival question.

Perhaps, then, the decision confronting us has as much to do with values and intentions as with scientific resourcefulness. Do we really care what death "is"? Does it matter whether or not there is survival after death and, if so, of what type? I am inclined to believe that many of us *do* care about these questions, but are not keen about admitting it. The questions seem hopelessly old-fashioned and perhaps beyond answer no matter what. These are good reasons for keeping our latent interest in the survival question well under wraps. It may not be the most significant reason, however. Science often has been fueled by passion. It has not been just "idle curiosity," although that has played its constructive role, or pragmatic enterprise (to build a more lethal weapon system or win power, fame, fortune). There have been people intensely motivated by the passion to discover, to know, to understand. This is neither an "objective" nor a tidy attitude. It is an orientation that tends to carry all before it, whether on a trail that proves fruitful or ends in error, even in disaster. Passion is not much in favor in the research establishment today. Technical craftmanship and "good behavior" receive more approbation and reward. Too bad! Too bad for our understanding of the really big questions! If we really care about the nature of life and death and can admit it to ourselves, this will not guarantee any success at all in either meditative or empirical ventures. But it is difficult to imagine even the prospect of success if we limit ourselves to picking politely around the edges of the problem in odd moments. Should we ever decide that we really want to know the answers we might get some place with the questions.

# References

Douglas, A., *Extrasensory powers*. New York: Overlook, 1976.

Garrett, E. J., *My Life as a Search for the Meaning of Mediumship*. London: Rider, 1939.

Garrett, E. J., *Many Voices: The Autobiography of a Medium*. New York: Putnam, 1968.

Gauld, A., "Discarnate Survival," in B. B. Wolman, ed., *Handbook of Parapsychology*. New York: Van Nostrand Reinhold, 1977, pp. 577–630.

Gurney, E., Podmore, F., and Myers, F. W. H., *Phantasms of the Living*. London: Trubner, 1886.

Hart, H., *The Enigma of Survival*. Springfield, Ill.: Charles C Thomas, 1959.

James, W. "Frederic Myers's Service to Psychology," in *Proceedings of the Society for Psychic Research*. London, 1901. Reprinted in G. Murphy and R. O. Ballou, eds., *William James on Psychical Research*. London: Chatto & Windus, 1961, pp. 213–224.

Kastenbaum, R., *Death, Society, and Human Experience*. St. Louis: C. V. Mosby, 1977.

Kastenbaum, R., and Aisenberg, R. B., *The Psychology of Death*. New York: Springer, 1972.

Lee, J. Y., *Death and Beyond in the Eastern Perspective*. New York: Interface, 1974.

Myers, F. W. H., *Human Personality and Its Survival of Bodily Death*. 2 vols. London: Longmans, 1903. Reprinted, New York: Arno Press, 1975.

Osis, K., *Deathbed Observations by Physicians and Nurses*. New York: Parapsychology Foundation, 1961.

Osis, K., and Haraldsson, E., *At the Hour of Death*. New York: Avon, 1977.

Owen, I. M., and Sparrow, M., *Conjuring Up Philip*. Toronto: Fitzhery & Whitseely, 1976.

Parkes, C. M., *Bereavement*. New York: International Universities Press, 1972.

Salter, W. H., *Zoar: The Evidence of Psychical Research Concerning Survival*. London: Sidgwick & Jackson, 1961.

Saltmarsh, H. F., *Evidence of Personal Survival from Cross Correspondences*. London: G. Bell, 1938. Reprinted, New York: Arno Press, 1975.

Schmeidler, G., "Quantitative Investigation of a Haunted House," *Journal of the American Society for Psychical Research*, 1966, 60, 137–149.

Sidgwick, E. B., "Notes on the Evidence, Collected by the Society, for Phantasms of the Dead," in *Proceedings of the Society for Psychic Research*. London, 1885, 3, 69–150.

Sidgwick, E. B., and Committee, "Report on the Census of Hallucinations," in *Proceedings of the Society for Psychic Research*. London, 1894, 10, 25–422.

Stevenson, I., *Twenty Cases Suggestive of Reincarnation*. 2nd ed. Charlottesville, Va.: University of Virginia Press, 1974.

Stevenson, I., "The Explanatory Value of the Idea of Reincarnation," *Journal of Nervous and Mental Disease*, 1977, 164, 305–326.

Tyrrell, G. N. M., *Apparitions*. New York: Macmillan, 1962.